OTHER BOOKS AUTHORED BY DR OLERIBE INCLUDE

- Repositioning for Marital Success
- Celebrating Marital Success
- Scaling New Heights
- Transforming Ideas, Seed for Entrepreneurship and Greatness
- Vital Leadership Thoughts and Nuggets
- The Concept of Child Abuse
- Fundamentals of Child Rights
- ADJS at 40: Celebrating Excellence, Consolidating the Vision (Editor)

MAKING MAXIMUM
IMPACT IN
LIFE
THE KEYS

OBINNA OSITADIMMA OLERIBE

authorHOUSE®

AuthorHouse™
1663 Liberty Drive
Bloomington, IN 47403
www.authorhouse.com
Phone: 1 (800) 839-8640

Published by AuthorHouse 11/27/2019

ISBN: 978-1-7283-3596-4 (sc)
ISBN: 978-1-7283-3594-0 (hc)
ISBN: 978-1-7283-3595-7 (e)

Library of Congress Control Number: 2019918672

Print information available on the last page.

Any people depicted in stock imagery provided by Getty Images are models, and such images are being used for illustrative purposes only.
Certain stock imagery © *Getty Images.*

Scripture quotations marked KJV are from the Holy Bible, King James Version (Authorized Version). First published in 1611. Quoted from the KJV Classic Reference Bible, Copyright © *1983 by The Zondervan Corporation.*

This book is printed on acid-free paper.

DEDICATED

In Memory of my father, Mr. Wilfred Nwadike Oleribe
and
My Mother, Mrs. Mercy Ure Oleribe

They gave me the fundamental key of Life that
started everything. Thank you for the price
you paid to have me, nurture and train me
and help me become the man I am today

CONTENTS

Acknowledgement ix
Preamble xi

Part 1: Introduction xiii

Chapter 1:   Let Me Start By Saying 1
Chapter 2:   Why Keys 6
Chapter 3:   The Keys of the Kingdom 9

Part 2: Fundamental Keys 19

Chapter 4:   Discovery 23
Chapter 5:   Revelation 32
Chapter 6:   Believe 40
Chapter 7:   Salvation 49
Chapter 8:   Reconciliation 59

Part 3: Enhancing Keys 67

Chapter 9:   Confession 69
Chapter 10: Positive Thinking 82
Chapter 11: The Fruit of the Spirit 92
Chapter 12: Joy 102

Chapter 13: Peace 114
Chapter 14: Patience... 126
Chapter 15: Gentleness.. 135
Chapter 16: Goodness 139
Chapter 17: Faith... 144
Chapter 18: Meekness 159
Chapter 19: Self-Control... 168
Chapter 20: Holy Spirit 180
Chapter 21: Ask... 195
Chapter 22: Kingdom Service 204
Chapter 23: Kingdom Service (Part 2).....................215

Part 4: Prosperity Keys.. 227

Chapter 24: Offerings... 233
Chapter 25: Offerings (Part 2) 244
Chapter 26: Tithes... 253
Chapter 27: Sacrifice... 258
Chapter 28: Thanksgiving....................................... 264
Chapter 29: Take a Chance....................................271
Chapter 30: Until You are Saved, You are Not Safe... 278

When.. 283
Epilogue: Let's Keep in Touch................................. 287
About the Author.. 289

ACKNOWLEDGEMENT

As my Bishop will always say, "Every professor is a product of references." This work could not have been possible but for the help of the Holy Spirit coupled with life impacting and insightful teachings of my various Pastors over the years. I therefore thank Bishop David Abioye and Dayo Olutayo, Pastors Dele Bamgboye, Paul Michael Onyebuchi, Folu Coker, Triumphant Obamoh, Okenwa Nwagu, Ike Ihuoma, Joseph Ajibade, Chris Abraham, and many others whom God has used tremendously to establish and nourish me in the faith.

I also appreciate my wife, Princess Olivia Ifunanya Osita-Oleribe, who has been on my side these eighteen years. I celebrate my children: Alpha Chimgozirim, Delight Chimziterem and Winner Chimkaneme Osita, the infallible proofs of God's faithfulness and love.

I thank Chisom O Anukam, Uloma Maduforo, Chikadibia MaryJane Anike and all others who spent their valuable time to review, edit, and improve the quality of this book. Finally, I extend my thanks to my friends and associates across the nations of the world who have positively impacted my life on various fronts.

God bless you all.

PREAMBLE

I have looked into the activities of men, and I discovered that, reading removes rust, studying stabilizes situations, and learning liberates lives.

This book started on the 25th of November 2001, when God instructed me, saying

"What you hear, write it down, that they may run with it that readeth it. Do not keep it all to yourself."

God always has a purpose for any and everything. My prayer is that this book will assist you reach your high places in life, as well as help change your life, and put you in charge.

I urge you to take this book as a major force that God has brought your way towards establishing your dominion on earth. Read it, reflect on your new findings, advise yourself and do what the book expects you to do per time. Do not neglect any God given instruction. It is in doing what you are asked to do that profiting will come, not merely in reading.

Keys are critical to success. It takes applying the right key to have dominion over the lock. In this kingdom, there are no master keys as every key answers to a particular issue, problem or desire.

I pray that this book will yield unto you all that the Father, the Son, and the Holy Spirit had laid in stock for you. It is not just an ordinary book. Read it with expectation, asking for the assistance of the great teacher – the Holy Spirit. As you eat up the fresh menu contained in this book, I see God placing in your hands all the keys that you require for kingdom excellence. Shalom.

PART ONE

INTRODUCTION

"You never have a second chance
for first impressions."

This book is about to open your eyes to your position in the covenant, your rights, privileges and opportunities. However, to obtain them, you need a good understanding of what keys are and how to use them. In this introductory section, I will be explaining what I mean by keys, so that we can understand each other throughout this book. I will also highlight the four basic keys found in the Bible. I expect you to fix each of the keys we will be discussing subsequently into any of these four keys. Happy reading.

CHAPTER ONE

LET ME START BY SAYING

"Sin procures death and destructions; Salvation procures decorations and distinctions"

I strongly believe that why many people are suffering, despite the fact that they may be born again – sometimes for several years – is because they lack understanding of their place in God, the reason for their calling, the provisions of God for their lives, the important part they must play to attain their high places in life, the hindrances they must deal with in order to truly enjoy life, and the reality of divine abundance / prosperity / provisions, health, joy, peace and of God's everlasting faithfulness. These are some of the major reasons why today, many Christians are asked on daily basis by their mockers, 'where is your God?'

Having been a full partaker of the promises of God since my conversion several years ago, and a daily beneficiary of the teachings of great men of God, especially, from the Living Faith Church (Winners' Chapel), I deem it a duty to share some kingdom discoveries with all believers,

1

believing that as you read and do what you are asked to do, you too shall be a wonder to your generation.

Ignorance is an obstacle.

What you do not know is your mountain, and the things you do not see are the reasons why you may be facing that ordeal right now. On my way back from church one day, I stopped at a friend's house; he is a technician. I complained to him about my air-conditioner which became faulty suddenly and I could not fix it. He just walked into my room, looked at the air-conditioner, went outside, and few seconds later, the air-conditioner started working. A miracle you will say. No, it was not a miracle. It was knowledge at work.

He just went out and checked the fuse box, and discovered that the switch to the air-conditioner tripped off. He put it back in the 'on' position, and like someone in a dream, the thing is back cooling my room again.

I was not able to do what he did, and suffered all this while for such a minor problem because I lacked the right knowledge. You know, when I asked him what happened, he just smiled and reminded me that I cannot be a doctor and an electrician at the same time. Then I gave up.

Why am I including this little experience in this book? Just because it came at the right time and goes on to buttress what I am about to say. The major reason why God's people are suffering is not because Satan has suddenly become too powerful or there are now more ferocious and killer demons attacking the sons of God. No, rather it is because they lack the requisite knowledge of how to make it in life, what to do to change their present circumstances, where to go for a divine touch, how to open the doors of blessings God has put right in front of them, and even knowledge of whose report to believe, when to take a step and when to just trust God.

No wonder God said **"My people are destroyed for lack of knowledge: …" in Hosea 4:6 KJV**. To emphasize what He meant in the above statement, He re-iterated in Isaiah 5:13 KJV

"Therefore, my people are gone into captivity, because they have no knowledge: and their honorable men are famished, and their multitude dried up with thirst: Therefore, hell hath enlarged herself, and opened her mouth without measure: and their glory, and their multitude, and their pump, and he that rejoiceth, shall descend into it. And the mean man shall be brought down, and the mighty man shall be humbled, and the eyes of the lofty shall be humbled:"

This is the price of ignorance – destruction! Ignorance is a major stumbling block to divine distinction. It brings about hunger and starvation, barrenness, frustration, sorrow, depression, failures, career crisis, humiliations, and sometimes, untimely deaths. Maybe you too have suffered many things in the hands of your enemies, or even in your business and or career because of the same reason. But I see the situation changing now for you for good, and God's glory descending to decorate you and your destiny, amen.

3

Ignorance is not an excuse.

In the kingdom, ignorance is not an excuse; actually, it is the only mountain before you. It could have been permitted as an excuse when you were not yet born again and the things you did then, God overlooked. However, after repentance, you need knowledge to successfully make it in the kingdom. Where you refuse knowledge, destruction is inevitable.

This is why He went on to say in Hosea 4:6b KJV, **"because thou has rejected knowledge, therefore have I rejected you"**. My prayer this day is that you shall not reject knowledge, but rather seek and 're-seek' it until you find it; and when you must have found it, preserve it in your heart, because in knowledge is life, power and strength; and from it wisdom is gotten.

Why this book?

This book will help you understand your place in God and what you need to do to remain or become a kingdom star. I rely completely on the Holy Spirit to help me convey the information in a way that you will not only love to read it, but also in an easy and understandable fashion. I pray that our great and excellent teacher and helper, the Holy Spirit will grant you understanding and deep insight into the things of God. The devil has cheated you too long, that must stop.

Pray this prayer with me;

God, grant that your Holy Spirit will help me read with understanding, so that my life will become outstanding, and all generation shall call me blessed. Amen.

I sincerely pray that, as you read this book, and as insight comes upon you, God shall wipe away all your secret tears in Jesus name, amen.

See you at the top.

CHAPTER TWO

WHY KEYS

"All doors remain locked until the right key is applied;
a locked destiny-door blocks a glorious destiny"

Keys connote solutions. In every place where treasures
are stored, a good lock is always put in place to secure
the treasures. To this end, only those that have the key or
keys to the store, have access to the secured treasures.

Likewise, what is required to make maximum impact in life
is kept securely in a spiritual mansion. The locks on the
door cannot be broken; neither can anyone enter through
the windows. The only way one can have access to these
treasures is through the door, and only those that have the
right key(s) can enter and obtain.

Having a key, however, is not enough; having the right key
is what matters. For instance, while tithing and sowing of
seed is one of the keys to financial prosperity (Gen: 8:22),
prayer and fasting is a vital key towards the destruction of
yokes, loosening of burdens, and end of wickedness (Is:

58:6). Only the right key can grant you access to the riches of God and His provisions. No wonder Jesus said,

"And I will give unto thee the keys of the kingdom of heaven: and whatsoever you bind on earth shall be bound in heaven: and whatsoever thou shalt loose on earth shall be loosed in heaven." (Lk: 16:19).

See, He says keys. In other words, He is saying that there are many keys to an impactful life. With the keys, you bind what you do not like or loose what you desire. Any of these keys you discover and apply effectively will yield unto you kingdom surprises and testimonies.

Notice that He did not say a 'key', but 'keys'. That means that there are more than one key, a separate key for a particular issue of life. A discovery of these keys is the first step towards total recovery of all that the devil has stolen from you.

A good understanding of how to apply these keys effectively is the second vital step towards excellent kingdom life, and a proper application of them results in wonderful kingdom breakthroughs – in all areas of life.

Until you discover these keys therefore, your struggles continue. Look at an account in Judges 3:15-25, Ehud after killing Eglon the king of Moab, shut the doors of the parlor upon him, locked them, and left.

The Devil also uses the same method against believers. Due to believers' ignorance of divine provisions, the devil shuts several doors of life against them. And maybe like

7

the servants of Eglon, you are assuming that it is God or even destiny that has locked you out, and all this while, you have been tarring outside the door until you are ashamed, waiting for the doors to open, but they have not yet opened. I have good news for you. Do what they did and walk into your miracle.

The Bible recorded that when he opened not the door, **"they took the key, and opened them"**. Notice that they just took the key. This means that all this time, while they were waiting outside the door, they had the key. You too have the keys of life. God designed them, gave them to us at salvation, but many are yet to use their own keys. Many are tarring outside their inheritance. Today, as you discover and use the appropriate keys, I see you walking into your inheritance in God.

Many do not even know that these keys exist. To others, the devil has blinded their eyes to these keys. This book will remove the veil over your eyes and then you shall see, use, and reap the resultant benefits arising from the proper use of these keys.

CHAPTER THREE

THE KEYS OF THE KINGDOM

"Behind every closed door are hidden
treasures; discovering and applying the
right keys reveal these treasures."

There are four major and cardinal keys mentioned in the bible for maximum impact in life and ministry. I will speak briefly on them here so you can understand that even God uses keys to achieve His objectives.

When the need arises, He employs the services of a key to solve a problem. Remember Jesus Christ told us that as His father has sent Him, so He has sent us. To achieve the same kind of results God the father is obtaining, to manifest as Jesus Christ manifested while on earth, we must follow their examples, and implant our footprints in the impression made by theirs.

Among these keys are;

1. **The key of Knowledge**: There is a key of knowledge. To access good and adequate knowledge, one needs this vital key. Jesus Christ speaking in Luke 11:52, made mention of this key when He said, **"for you have taken away the key of knowledge".**

   You see every believer ought to have access to this key; but it could be taken away, especially if you lack understanding of its existence and usefulness. What you do not know that you have, you may never use, and you can easily lose.

   The key of knowledge is the Word of God. Everything you need to know about life, challenges, temptations, successes, prosperity, divine distinction, career exploits, etc. are all available in this Word of life. It is the manual provided by the maker for the effective use of His product, which is man. The Bible speaking on the daily situations faced by man said, **"The things that hath been, it is that which shall be; and that which is done is that which shall be done: and there is no new thing under the earth." (Eccl 1:9).** The devil also knows this. However, the devil may deceive you into not understanding the importance of this key and thus not using it.

   For instance, the devil may cause you not to believe in the Word of God and/or make you to call it all manner of names. He may even prevent you from reading it as often as is required. He may make you use it wrongly, thereby preventing you from obtaining the benefits of using the key. Whichever one is your problem, as you discover your place in God, I see you taking back what is rightly yours in the kingdom.

Jesus understood this very possibility, and that was why he was sad that they took away the key of knowledge and rebuked them because like the devil, **"ye entered not in yourselves, and them that were entering in ye hindered."** Why? Because **"ye shut up the kingdom of heaven *(with the keys ye took away)* against men:" (Mt 23:13).**

When your key is taken away, access is completely denied. And frustrations and suffering manifest. I, therefore, pray today that as you read this book, "The eyes of your understanding" will be enlightened, that you will know what is the hope of His calling, and what the riches of the glory of His inheritance in the saints are through the full discovery and efficient utilization of the keys I will be discussing from the next chapter (Eph 1:18).

This key of knowledge can open several life transforming doors and gates. For instance, when one understands adequately the operational modalities and faithfully practices the covenant of tithing and offering, the key opens for him the windows of heaven and a lot of blessings are then released upon him. Therefore, the Word said,

"Bring ye all the tithes into the store house, that there may be meat in mine house, and prove me now herewith, saith the Lord of hosts, if I will not open you windows of heaven, and pour you out a blessing, that there shall not be room enough to receive it. And I shall rebuke the devourer for your sake, and he shall not destroy the fruits of your ground; neither shall your vine cast her fruits before the time in the field, saith the Lord of hosts." (Mal 3:10-11). When He must have done this, then **"all nations *(of the earth)* shall call you blessed: for ye shall be a delightsome land *(person)*, saith the Lord of hosts." (Vs. 12).** Thus the key of knowledge is the escape route from all the pollutions and defilements of our world. Here is what Apostle Peter said,

"For if after we have escaped the pollutions of the world through the knowledge of the Lord and Saviour Jesus Christ, they are again entangled therein, and overcome, the later end is worse with them than the beginning." (2 Pet 2:20). Having access to this vital key and losing it again leads to a more disastrous end. That shall never be your portion till eternity.

Therefore, I urge you to guard and protect this vital key jealously from all enticements of the enemy that your end be not a disappointment, **"for it had been better for them *(you)* not to have known the way of righteousness *(through this key)*, than, after** they *(you)* have known it, to turn from the holy commandment delivered unto them *(you).*"

May it never be said of you that **"the dog is turned to his own vomit again; and the sow that was washed to her wallowing in the mire." (Vs.21-22).**

2. **The Key of the bottomless pit**: The earth is full of evil. Beside every great work of God, there are several challenges. The wider the gate that God opens, the bigger the adversaries against it. There is nothing God has said that the enemy will not contest. These challenges come in diverse ways. Only one with a true knowledge of the operations of God can effectively avoid or handle these challenges.

The bottomless pit represents the place of the demons and of Satan, the Prince of demons (Rev 9:11). In this pit are all the horrible things of life – poverty, diseases, infirmity, barrenness, nakedness, death, accidents, misfortunes, mishaps, marital problems, etc. The devil is always trying to lure God's children into this pit. But I have good news for you. There is a key to this pit. In Revelation 9:1 it is written,

"And the fifth angel sounded, and I saw a star fall from heaven unto the earth: and to him was given the key of the bottomless pit."

This key which is usually kept by Christ, was temporarily given to this fallen angel (Rev 1:17&18).

For the unsaved, the devil is still holding the keys to their bottomless pits.

When Christ died, the Bible said that He descended to hell and one of the things He took from Satan was this key. He took it from him to protect the believers from the grief and sorrows of the bottomless pit. At salvation, by giving your life to Jesus Christ, you made a choice to allow Christ keep this key for you. When the door is tightly and properly locked by Jesus Christ, all the fruits of Satan are kept far away from you. This is what Christ is doing for all His children.

But many are ignorant of this. So, they unknowingly break the hedge. When you break the hedge through sin, disobedience, wrong confessions, doubts, etc., Satan may temporarily have access to this key again and work against you. When he does, he opens the door of the pit. If you allow Satan to keep the door open, then you become a victim and servant to these problems.

What makes the difference, therefore, between one believer and another is this knowledge. I see you making the right choice now for Christ, standing regularly on the covenant so that He will not only keep the key, but will also lock this door everlastingly for you.

3. **The keys of hell and death**: These are very vital keys in the kingdom. Only Christ holds this key. Knowledge of this by all, especially unbelievers,

is important. All have sinned and come short of the glory of God. Our sins have convicted and sentenced us, but Jesus Christ holds these keys.

He alone can free us from eternal bondage, and damnation. He alone has the power to set us free from the power of sin and death. At salvation, we registered for this freedom, and as such need not have to fear hell or death because our redeemer, Jesus Christ holds the key that leads to both.

However, the case is different for unbelievers. When people disregard God, and try to control their lives, they set a course that leads directly to hell. All they do in their attempt for self-justification and self-righteousness is similar to obeying a set of instructions like a robot, which is tele-guided by a higher force – the devil. This sets in motion a course of activities that finally leads to hell.

But when one places his life in the hands of Jesus, He restores him back, and puts things in place that will ensure eternal and peaceful life after resurrection. No wonder Christ, speaking in John 10:10 said:

"The thief cometh not, but for to steal, and to kill, and to destroy: I am come that they might have life, and that they might have it more abundantly."

Christ came to give us life here and hereafter, make sure that nothing works against us, prevent the destructive plans of Satan from affecting our glorious destiny, and protect our colourful and bright tomorrow. However, only those that have accepted Him have access to His ministry. If you have not yet accepted Him as your Lord and personal Saviour, this is the time to do just that. Kindly turn to the last page of this book and pray the sinners' prayer, and God will forgive you all your sins, cancel your name from the book of death, and restore you to your rightful place in Christ.

4. **The key of David**: This key is also called the key of opportunities. Once you are saved by believing in God and confessing Jesus Christ as your Lord and personal saviour, you are then **entitled** to this key. This is the key that opens the door leading to the benefits of salvation, which includes divine provisions, total health, all round fruitfulness, peace, joy, etc.

Once this door is opened, no devil can close it –if you walk in the covenant– and salvation is assured. However, you can shut this door against yourself when you sin against God. Once the door is closed, only total repentance and forsaking of evil ways can re-open it, otherwise it shall remain permanently locked and at the end of time, judgment is certain.

The key of David, therefore, represents Christ's authority to open the door of invitation into His future kingdom. And only the eligible can enter. Confirming that this key is with Jesus, Isaiah prophesied,

"And the key of the house of David will I lay upon His shoulder: so He shall open, and none shall shut: and He shall shut, and none shall open." (Is 22:22).

Only the person that has access to this key (through salvation) has access to the things in the house of David – the treasures of darkness, and the hidden riches of secret places – which are reserved for them that love God.

Your acceptance of Jesus today makes you a bonafide beneficiary of these riches. However, your rejection of Christ exempts you from the riches. The choice is yours, and the choice you make now determines whether you will benefit from this book or not as only those that are in Christ have access to divine secrets, which are what this book is all about.

What else do you need to know?

This book will be revealing to us how to find and use the treasures in the house of David. The moment you confess Jesus Christ as your Lord and personal saviour, the doors into the house of David are opened to you. But only those that have access to the keys can open the boxes, lockers, drawers, and cabinets and partake fully of the riches in the house.

Knowledge of these keys and their judicious use is what makes one Christian different from the other. For behind the rise of any star is a secret – he knows what others do not know, he discovered what others have not yet discovered, and he implements what others are yet to implement.

Do you not know that great men do frequently what common men do not do (or rarely do)? It is secrets that make a man. This book will be providing you with those secret keys. One thing the enemy cannot handle is the light of God's word. As you encounter them in this book, I see all your misery turned into masteries.

PART TWO

FUNDAMENTAL KEYS

"Your foundation determines your future; the
stronger your foundation, the better your future."

**If the foundations be destroyed, what can the righteous
do? (Ps 11:3).** The nature of the foundation of a building
determines the kind of building that will be erected. If a
skyscraper is your desire, then a very strong and deep
foundation is all you need. However, in case you want to
build a batcher, a foundation may not be necessary.

But to be a kingdom star, you need a solid foundation.
This makes you unmovable when the storms of life arise.
Challenges must arise. The question is when? The prophet
Isaiah speaking on this issue said,

**"When thou passeth through the waters, I will be
with thee; and through the rivers, they shall not over
flow thee: when thou walkest through the fire, thou
shall not be burned; neither shall the flame kindle
upon thee." (Is 43:2).** He did not say 'if' but 'when'. When
these prophesied challenges appear, your foundation will

determine the outcome – whether you will remain on top or change to the bottom. If you have a solid foundation, you are preserved. Otherwise you perish. This was why Jesus, speaking to His disciples, said;

"...a wise man...built his house upon a rock: And the rain descended, and the floods came, and the winds blew, and beat upon the house; and it fell not: for it was founded upon a rock *(a solid foundation).* On the other hand,

...a foolish man...built his house upon the sand: And the rain descended, and the floods came, and the wind blew, and beat upon the house; and it fell: and great was the fall of it." (Mt 7:24-27).

The difference between a wise man and a foolish man from this passage is the nature of their foundations. Wisdom is essential for maximum impact, therefore, only wise men with solid foundations are qualified to enjoy kingdom excellence. This is why we will start this journey with the fundamental or foundational keys. They will help enlighten your paths as when the foundation is destroyed, darkness becomes inevitable. See what the Psalmist has to say,

"They know not, neither will they understand; they walk in darkness: *(because)* **all the foundations of the earth** *(their lives)* **are out of course." (Ps 82:5).**

When your foundation is out of course, stumbling, stagnation and frustration are inevitable.

May this book help you to know and understand your place in the kingdom; assist you build a solid foundation so that your life may become full of light; remove the veil from off your face and enhance your vision so that you may not stumble again. May you be among the wise ones in Christ as you take steps to develop an enviable foundation.

CHAPTER FOUR

DISCOVERY

"What you fail to discover, you cannot recover."

In life, most good things have coverings over them. The gold is covered by the earth, likewise the crude oil and similar natural resources. Egg has a shell cover; the delicious part of an orange and other fruits have bitter coverings.

Treasures are usually hidden. Until the cover is removed, access to these sweet things of life is hindered. For instance, no matter how much gold a nation is blessed with, until the earth is removed and the gold excavated, it remains useless to the people. But, the day it is discovered, life takes a new meaning for everyone. So, it is the day one discovers him/herself that his/her destiny and his purpose in life is unveiled.

I will like to define discovery simply as, **"the *destruction* of every *covering* masking ones inheritance in God"**. That is, '**to destroy the covering**'. Until the covering over any thing is destroyed, the real beauty is not seen, the value is not appreciated, and proper use is hindered. In such cases, abuses are inevitable.

It is the Lord that opens our eyes.

True discovery is of God. The Lord Himself is always helping us discover ourselves by destroying every covering or veil over our destinies, future, heritage and treasures. This is one of the key benefits of going to church – the mountain of the Lord. Hear what Isaiah said;

"And in this mountain *(the church of God)* **shall the Lord of hosts make unto all people a feast of fat things, a feast of wines on the lees, of fat things full of marrow, of wines on the lees well refined. And He will destroy in this mountain the face of the covering cast over all people, and the veil that is spread over all nations. He will swallow up death in victory; and the Lord will wipe away tears from off all faces; and the rebuke of His people shall He take away from off all the earth:" (Is 25:6-8).**

Why discovery?

Discovery helps us to know who we are, what our destinies hold in stock for us, and our rights in the covenant. What you do not know, you cannot understand; what you cannot understand, you may never desire; what you do not desire, you do not deserve; what you do not deserve, you cannot receive; and what you do not receive, you cannot enjoy. In other words, it is what the eyes see and understand that the heart yields itself to seek.

Discovery uncovers our destiny. Destiny undiscovered is never celebrated, and if they remain uncelebrated, life may become full of struggles and frustrations.

Discovery, they say, is the mother of recovery. Discovering who you are, what you are meant to be, what God has destined you for, why the enemy is always challenging, and how to re-write your history and arrive at your Canaan, is a must for exceptional manifestation and kingdom exploits.

Today, many Christians are suffering because they do not know what provisions God has made for their freedom; some even believe that they must have to pass through what they are passing through as part of their cross, some take it that tribulations, suffering, and frustrations are part of everyday living. Others still believe that God may be punishing them for their sins, lack of faith, or even what they did before becoming Christians – that is, before giving their lives to God. But these are not the cases.

Let me state categorically here that the reason why many are suffering is because they are yet to discover what God has prepared and reserved for them from the foundation of the earth. Challenges are real, victory over them has already been won by Christ. Did you not see it in the passage read above? The word said that once the covering cast over the faces of all the people and the veil spread over all the nations are removed, death will be swallowed up in victory, tears and shame will be wiped away, and all afflictions and trials shall be taken away.

Discovering, therefore, your place in God is a primary kingdom key for kingdom excellence and maximum impact in life.

Until you discover whose child you are, you cannot enjoy your heritage; until you discover what gifts you have, you cannot use them for your celebration and enhancement; until you discover what provisions have been made available for your escape, you remain in bondage; until you discover how to move forward, you remain stagnated; and until you discover the reason why you are alive, your life remains meaningless.

Discovery, therefore, is the bedrock of all kingdom exploits, for **"the people that do know their God *(i.e. Have discovered their place in God)* shall be strong and do exploits." (Dan 11:32)**

Look at this case for instance. One man was born to the wealthiest person in his city. However, while he was yet very young, following a quarrel with his father, his mother took him to a faraway land. All through life, the woman told this boy that his father was dead. They had to feed from hand to mouth because things were very tough for them. Poverty was their middle name. Friends made jest of the young man because of their poverty and his fatherlessness.

Schooling was stopped due to his mother's inability to pay his school fees. Things became so bad that they had to live in ramshackle because that was the only shelter they could afford. While they were in this state, his father (who never re-married) died when he was barely fifteen and willed everything he had to him – being his only child.

He did not know about this inheritance until twenty – five years later. This he found out of curiosity. He was going through his mother's documents one day when he discovered where his mother wrote that a certain man was his father. That documentation has been there for close to thirty years, but he never saw it. He then confronted his mother, whom in-between tears told him the story of his life. This young man set out in search of his father, only to discover that his father died 25 years earlier. Not willing to give up, he went in search of the relations. That was when he discovered that he was actually a very rich man and the rightful occupant of the throne. His story then changed. His discovery changed his situation.

Many people today are suffering because they have failed to, like the man in the story above, discover their true heritage. The fact that you have a glorious heritage is not all that matters. What matters more is your discovery of this heritage and how to appropriate it to yourself. I see you discovering your true heritage in Christ and manifesting your true nature.

Like the prodigal son in the Bible, many Christians are eating the food meant for pigs while servants in their fathers' houses are feeding fat. But as we discover and re-discover ourselves, I see the situation changing for good for all of us. Discovery always precedes recovery.

The children of Israel were in captivity in Egypt for four hundred and thirty years. As long as the captivity was convenient for them, they remained in it. But when they discovered that they had a better heritage and cried to God, God came down and sent Moses to Pharaoh. After some demonstrations of power, one night their freedom was restored, their captivity turned, and their wages for all the years they were in captivity paid. They had enough resources for a forty year-long journey. Why? They discovered their true heritage.

Peter and his fellow fishermen were all out into the high sea in Luke Chapter 5 fishing. Throughout the night, they caught nothing. They had the qualifications, the experience, the expertise, and knew where and when fishes could be caught in the sea. But this night, despite their training and all, they caught nothing. However, when they discovered, through Jesus, that they have been fishing in shallow waters, that the rules had changed, and that fishes had changed their habitation, they launched out into the deep and what a great draught that followed. The fish they caught nearly tore their net. But it was the same river where they had been all night. Above all, the time was to them very wrong. But still, they had a boat sinking, net breaking draught. Why? They just discovered, accepted their mistakes and ignorance, and took a step based on knowledge. Today as you do the same, I see you too reaping a mind-blowing harvest.

This same Peter had another encounter with Jesus. With his men, he went fishing in John chapter 21, and all through the night, they caught nothing, not knowing that they had been fishing on the *wrong side* all night. But when they discovered their mistakes, again through the Master – Jesus, and obeyed His instruction to cast their net on the *right side* of the ship, they had a great catch and the Bible recorded,

"and now they were not able to draw it for the multitude of fishes." (Jn 21:6).

As you discover what you have done wrong or failed to do, and take the necessary steps to correct it, I see total restoration coming your way now in Jesus mighty name, Amen.

There was also another man in the Bible called Naaman. This man had a wonderful credential, however, there was a *'but'* in his life.

"Now Naaman, captain of the host of the king of Syria, was a great man with his master, and honourable, because by him the LORD had given deliverance unto Syria: he was also a mighty man in valour, *but he was a leper.*" (2 Kings 5:1).

Through his servant, he discovered that healing was possible, that his circumstance was not terminal but could be reversed. So, he set out to make it happen. And after he dealt with pride and did what he was instructed to do, the reproach he had suffered for years was wiped away at little or no cost to him. The same is still possible for you. If only you can do what they did, so shall all your reproaches be wiped away, in Jesus name, amen.

Another example of discovery that changed a man's situation in the Bible is the prodigal son. I have mentioned him earlier in this discussion. However, whenever I think about him, I learn something new. Let me, therefore, share this one with you. In Luke 15:11-32, Jesus told us this parable. This son of a very rich man had every right to request for his inheritance from his father – as we all have – but he riotously wasted his inheritance – as some of us still do – and then started suffering. It got so bad that he sustained himself on stolen pigs' food. He could not return home because he was proud – what will people say – ignorant of his father's large heart, and unaware of his permanent place in the house of his father. However, the Bible recorded,

"And when he came to himself, he said…I will arise and go to my father, and will say unto him, Father, I have sinned against heaven, and before thee…. And he arose, and came to his father." (Lk 15:17-20).

The passage said 'when he came to himself'. This literally means 'when he discovered himself'. Many people are still today in their far country where there is famine and they are suffering because they have failed to come to themselves, that is, discover themselves. But as you discover yourself today, arise and take a step in obedience to the word of God, I prophesy total recovery of all that the devil has denied you and even a full restoration of the lost years and materials.

Benefits of discovery.

Discovery brings about;

- ❖ Restoration.
- ❖ Decoration
- ❖ Recovery, and
- ❖ Exceptional exploits.

I see you stepping into your inheritance as you take steps to discover yourself, your talents, your inheritance, and your covenant duties.

Things you must discover.

What do you need to discover? You need to discover your true place and position in God, the road to your high places, the way to divine health and trouble-free life, the provisions for deliverance, fruitfulness, prosperity, fame, glory, etc. It is your personal discoveries that will procure your recoveries. I will see you at the top.

Every true discovery is based on the scriptures. In all the above examples, Jesus was instrumental to their discoveries. The situation is still the same today. Jesus is the bedrock of all kingdom discoveries. And Jesus is the word of God, documented in the Bible. The Bible is the manual for discovery, neglecting the Bible results in lost destiny. It is the only avenue for lasting and real discoveries.

I present it to you today. Study it, meditate on it, believe in it, agree with it, confess it, and I see God opening your eyes to see what He has prepared for those who love Him.

CHAPTER FIVE

REVELATION

"Revelation releases elevations."

After you have discovered, you need to understand what you discovered and how to appropriate it to yourself before it can be useful to you.

All gold dug out from the earth has a thick veil of sand and other impurities on it. The crude oil has a lot of impurities too. So is our destiny in God. When we discover it, we need to unveil it to maximize its usefulness.

The young man who discovered his inheritance after so many years of suffering, now has all things and is very rich. However, most of the money his father had was lodged in different banks across the state. Therefore, for him to access these resources, he needed to know which banks his father used, what his bank numbers were and where he kept the will or authority to execute his estate. Then, backed with these materials, he could approach the banks to claim his inheritance. Without them, though the monies in the banks were truly his, his suffering will continue.

What am I saying? Discovery is important, but it is not all that is needed for kingdom exploits and maximum impact in life and ministry. You need revelation too!

What is revelation?

I will define revelation as **the process of *removing* the veil over your discovered inheritances.** That is, to completely unveil what you have discovered. Many people may know what their inheritances are in Christ Jesus, because they saw it in the Bible, but are still suffering. The Bible said that

"Not of the letter, but of the spirit: for the letter killeth, but the spirit giveth life." (2 Cor 3:6). It is not the discovery that makes for profiting; it is the understanding based on the revealed word of God by the Spirit of God that brings outstanding results. Jesus in John 6:63 said

"It is the Spirit that quickeneth: the flesh profiteth nothing: the words that I speak unto you, *they* are spirit, and *they* are life."

That is, until the spirit reveals the word and puts life into it, it profiteth nothing. To make this fact clearer, Paul in his letter to the Ephesians wrote

"The eyes of your understanding being enlightened: that ye may know what is the hope of His calling, and what the riches of the glory of His inheritance in the saints." (Eph 1:18). Thus, without enlightened eyes, one may never know what the discovered inheritance is, how to access it and what to do to make it completely his. Revelation, therefore, means understanding what you have just discovered in God.

Why revelation?

A single revelation may be all you need to achieve your goal on earth. The difference between one Christian and the other is their depth of understanding. Until it is revealed, it is still useless.

Many people are living below their standards because of absence of the revelation power of God, via the Holy Spirit. Revelation is your way out of depravity. Understanding your true self and realizing how to reach there is fundamental to total restoration and kingdom excellence and maximum impact.

For instance, how do you see yourself? Do you know that you are the bride of Christ?

As His bride, He cannot forsake you nor allow any evil to come your way that you cannot handle. Even before the evil is unveiled, He manifests himself. He will even go extra miles to make sure that nothing tampers with you.

However, you, as a bride must play your role. This is where revelation comes in. There are expectations from your bridegroom that you must meet to keep him happy and always be by your side. You know that some bridegrooms have forsaken their brides because of their brides' characters, attitudes and actions. This maybe because of ignorance of what is expected from her – the bride.

But as you allow the Holy Spirit to reveal to you God's expectations per time, I see God always assisting you to enjoy your inheritance in Christ.

Revelation is the prerequisite for revolution. Let us look at Jacob. While in his mother's womb, God chose him and rejected his brother Esau. But life was not easy for him. After coveting and receiving his brother's birthright and parental blessings, he ran away and stayed with his uncle, Laban. He served Laban for several years and within those years; Laban changed his wages ten times (Gen 31:7). However, a revelation from God made him a very wealthy man that even Laban became jealous of him.

Isaac, his father, also had a problem. After the death of Abraham, there arose a famine in the land where he was staying (Gen 26:1). Like his father, Isaac arose and wanted to run away, but God appeared to him. In the revelation, he was told not to go down to Egypt, but to sojourn in the land. He obeyed, and sowed in that land, and within the same year, he became an envy to a whole nation.

"And Isaac dwelt in Gerar...Then Isaac sowed in that land, and received in the same year an hundred fold: and the Lord blessed him. And the man waxed great, and went forward, and grew until he became very great...and the Philistines envied him." (Gen 26:6&12-14). He achieved this on the platform of revelation.

Daniel became mighty through revelation. When the king dreamed a dream and forgot the dream, he requested that his astrologers, magicians, sorcerers, and the Chaldeans both tell him the dream and its interpretation. He would have killed all (including Daniel and the three Hebrew boys) if Daniel had not had a revelation (Dan 2:19).

Zacharias, the father of John the Baptist, would have died a barren man if he had not had a revelation in the temple, while serving God (Lk 1:11-17).

Time will fail me to talk about Abraham, Moses, Joshua, Gideon, Jephthah, Deborah, and others, who through revelations became mighty, conquered nations, annihilated great kingdoms and engraved their names in the hall of fame of faith. When things seem not to be working, revelation of what to do, how to do it, when and where to do it is all you need.

I will never forget the testimony of a woman whose destiny was turned around through revelation. This woman and her husband were in dire financial need. They even lived in an abandoned building in a major town in Nigeria. However, when the word of God revealed to her the intentions of God concerning her situation, she went home and prayed a prayer of faith over her uncompleted building. Then things began to happen. First, a bank showed interest in the building and paid rent in advance. This financially empowered the husband of the woman of faith to complete the building. And today, they are landlords to a bank, a hospital and live in their own three-bedroom apartment.

Where does revelation come from?

True revelation comes only from God. Generally, God speaks to His children through His word. There is no closed case with God. With God, all things are possible. It may even seem impossible with men, but not with God. The word of God is capable of turning any situation around. Remember,

"He sent His word, and healed them, and delivered them from their destructions." (Ps 107:20). The word can heal all, deliver all, and save all, not some. The day revelation catches up with you, and the word brings light, you will be restored.

Do the right thing now.

Stop, therefore, running around looking for prayer contractors to pray for you and lay hands and legs on you; stop engaging in long and tiring prayer and fasting sessions. Revelation is the key you need. Prayer and fasting may help you hear God, but it is revelation that is the procurer of restoration. It is the bedrock of all restorations. Therefore, let the word of God dwell richly in you. Meditate on the word, eat the word, and obey the simple instruction, which said,

"Be thou strong and very courageous, that thou mayest observe to do according to all the law, which Moses my servant commanded thee: turn not from it to the right hand or to the left, that thou mayest prosper whithersoever thou goest." Furthermore, to emphasize the need to seek God for revelation through His word, it went on to add, **"This book of the law shall not depart out of thy mouth; but thou shalt meditate on it day and night, that thou mayest observe to do according to all that is written therein: for then thou**

shalt make thy way prosperous, and thou shall have good success. (Jos 1:7-8).

As you go all out for divine insight – called revelation – through a diligent search of scriptures, I see God restoring all your lost glory. And as you search into and meditate on the word of God, you shall in the final analysis enjoy fully all that salvation has to offer.

How does Revelation come from God?

God speaks to His children. Revelation comes through the voice of God. God spoke to our covenant fathers. He still speaks today, usually through the ministry of the Holy Spirit. Jesus said,

"My sheep hear my voice, and I know them, and they follow me:" (Jn 10:27). He did not say, 'my sheep heard my voice' but 'hear my voice'. Till date, His sheep still hear His voice. The spoken word is the revealed word of God. Sensitivity to the Spirit is therefore needed to maximize this avenue for kingdom excellence and maximum impact in life. Be sensitive to God and He will show you that which you ought to know.

God also speaks through His servants, the Prophets. Such declarations are generally referred to as Prophetic utterances. He said,

"Surely the Lord God will do nothing, but he revealeth his secrets unto his servants the prophets." (Amos 3:7). God usually uses the prophets as lively oracles to declare His counsel concerning His children. He loves speaking through His prophets, because He is the Lord **"That confirmeth the word of his servant, and performeth the counsel of his messengers;" (Is 44:26).** Once they speak, He puts mechanism in motion for fulfillment. He does not allow any of His words through their mouths to drop to the ground.

Finally, the Lord can also speak to His people through situations and circumstances. This is the type that is widely known, but poorly understood. It is very common to see a brother who has failed to secure a job for two to three years claim that the reason why he has failed to secure a good job is because God is calling him into the ministry. Or a sister who is aging without getting married to accept the lie of the devil that God is punishing her for the sins she committed, and another sister who is married but yet to conceive to believe that her predicament is because God is teaching her a lesson, maybe for abortions committed. When God speaks through an ongoing situation, it is usually very clear and easy to understand. This is because He is not an author of confusion.

Therefore, be sensitive to the Spirit, so that you do not miss out when the Spirit speaks to you.

When you hear Him, obey Him; otherwise He may stop speaking to you. This is very important as until you fully obey His previous instructions, God may not speak to you again. And as you obey Him, I see you eat the good of the land. (Is 1:19).

CHAPTER SIX

BELIEVE

"Believing brings faith, faith produces victory."

What you discovered or that has been revealed to you, if you do not believe, it is useless to you. Behind most sufferings in the kingdom is the sin of unbelief. No wonder Jesus said that when the Holy Spirit shall come,

"He will reprove the world of sin, and of righteousness, and of judgment: Of sin, because they believe not on me;"(Jn 16:8-9). The sin of unbelief, the Bible said, is like witchcraft.

Many Christians confess Christ with their mouths, but their hearts are full of unbelief. They say one thing but believe something else.

Let's go back to our story again. Even though our young friend has discovered his inheritance, and unveiled it, if he does not believe that he has the right to spend and use them, his suffering will continue. If he failed to believe that the throne is his or that the man that died is his father, he would have a long way to go.

40

Thus, the Word said;

"And blessed is she that believed: for there shall be a performance of those things which were told her from the lord." (Lk 1:45). There is no performance without first belief. In other words, where there is no belief, there is no performance.

"Jesus said unto him, If thou canst believe, all things are possible to him that believeth." (Mk 9:23). All things are possible, including kingdom excellence and making maximum impact in life, only to those that believe. Kingdom exploits is reserved for true believers, those that totally trust in God and in His words, thus Jesus said:

"For verily I say unto you, that whosoever shall say to this mountain, Be thou removed, and be thou cast into the sea; and shall not doubt in his heart, but shall believe that those things which he saith shall come to pass; he shall have whatsoever he saith." (Mk 11:23). Thus, only those that say, believing, have everything they said. What you do not believe, you cannot receive. It is only the believing Christian that can manifest the goodness of God. That is why the Bible said;

"But as many that received Him, to them gave He power to become the sons of God, even to them that believe on His name:" (Jn 1:12). You must first 'believe' to 'become'. To become anything in the kingdom, belief is a major pre-requisite. It is only those that believe that end up becoming kingdom stars – there is no shortcut.

Belief is it!

Unbelief is evil, devastating and a thief of destiny. The writer of Hebrews, emphasizing this fact said; **"Take heed, brethren, lest there be in any of you an evil heart of unbelief, in departing from the living God." (Heb 3:12).** He went on to say,

"Let us therefore fear, lest, a promise being left us of entering into His rest, any of you seem to come short of it. For unto us was the gospel preached, as well as unto them: but the word preached did not profit them, not being mixed with faith in them that heard it. For we which have believed do enter into rest. (Heb 4:1-3). If it is rest that you need, rest from the trials of the world, from the challenges of Satan, from the assaults of devil, from reproaches, shame, sicknesses, disappointments, unfruitfulness, wilderness experiences, curses, marital woes, etc., then belief is the key. Be not deceived, there is no other way out!

God is a God of principles. If he said, "To him that believeth, there shall be a performance", then that is exactly what He means. Do what He said, and reap what He promised. There is no shortcut.

Many people hear the word of God regularly, but it does not profit them, because the words they hear are not mixed with faith. If, therefore, you desire a change in your situation and you want to profit from the spoken and written word of God, you must be willing to believe it the way it is; whether it is convenient or not.

How to know the level of your belief.

This is what I call the evidence of belief. When your trust in God is total, this will manifest in

- ❖ Total obedience to His commands and instructions
- ❖ Rest on every side, knowing that what He has promised, He is also able to perform.
- ❖ Reverence for God's word and messengers, and their counsel
- ❖ Total reliance on God's ability, submitting everything to Him, knowing that he is too big and too powerful to mismanage your life.
- ❖ Asking for His opinion and guidance in everything that concerns you, knowing that He knows the end from the beginning; and
- ❖ Confessing regularly His promises and provisions.

There are great men and women in the Bible who dared to trust and believe God. By this singular step, their lives were transformed. I know that you can even mention a few of them – Abraham, Isaac, Jacob, Joseph, Gideon, Sarah, Deborah, etc. Please turn to the books of Hebrews, chapter 11 for a full list of these great and mighty men and women of God. However, let us look at some of them, see what they did and how we can learn from them.

Abraham was God's friend who chose to believe God rather than men. God called him when he was seventy-five years old to leave his father's house, kindred and country unto a land that He (God) will show him (Abraham) in Genesis Chapter 12:1. In verse 4 he departed, as the Lord had spoken to him, taking along with him his possessions, wife, nephew and others. Because he believed God, which was shown by his spontaneous and instantaneous obedience, God in verse 16 caused Pharaoh to entreat him well, thus he became a possessor of sheep, cattle, oxen, asses, camels and servants. And in the second verse of the very next chapter he became very rich in cattle, in silver and in gold. What a transformation. Believing, followed by total obedience to a command from God always result in amazing transformations.

God promised him a child (son), and for twenty-five years he waited without doubting, and the Bible said that it was imputed unto him for righteousness. Hear this,

"Therefore it is of faith...but to that also which is of the faith of Abraham; who is the father of us all, (As it is written, I have made thee a father of many nations), before whom he believed, even God...Who against hope believed in hope, that he might become the father of many nations, according to that which was spoken, so shall your seed be. And not being weak in faith, he considered not his own body now dead, when he was about an hundred years old, neither yet the deadness of Sarah's womb: He staggered not at the promises of God through unbelief; but was strong in faith, giving glory to God; And being fully persuaded that, what he had promised, he was able also to perform. And therefore it was imputed to him for righteousness." (Rom 4:16-22).

One is not therefore surprised, going by this degree of faith and belief that he was called a friend of God. Belief is the raw material for the development and nurturing of faith. Strong faith can only grow on the soil of total belief – being fully persuaded that come rain or sunshine, God is faithful. His belief and trust in God is still an exceptional example to all believers.

Look at how he ended,

"And Abraham was old, and well stricken in age: and the LORD *(who he dared to believe unequivocally)* **had blessed him in all things."** (Gen 24:1).

Daily, we sing and pray, "Abraham's blessings are mine". Although, we are his covenant children, we cannot obtain these blessings by just praying and singing about them. We must follow his examples to obtain the blessings. Since what God said to one, He says to another, and He is the same yesterday, today and forever, I see God making you His 'twenty-first century Abraham', as you dare to believe, even on His name.

The case of **Isaac** is about the same. In the time of famine when everyone was running away to places where there was greener pasture, he heard God in verse two of the twenty-six chapter of Genesis,

"And the LORD appeared unto him (Isaac), and said, Go not down into Egypt: dwell in the land which I shall tell thee of: Sojourn in the land, and I will be with thee..." (Gen 26:2-3).

Because he chose to believe God and stayed, planted and trusted God for increase, despite the famine and the hostility of the Philistines, God blessed him and in the same year, he reaped a hundredfold increase in harvest, and went on to become very great, that a whole nation –the same Philistines that antagonized him – envied him. As you chose this day to believe and rely on God, I see God making you an eternal Excellency and the joy of many generations.

Do you know what? Everything that was possible in Isaac is also possible in you, for the Bible says; **"Now we, brethren, as Isaac was, are the children of promise." (Gal 4:28).**

Even Joseph had a similar experience. The list is endless. What of Daniel and the three Hebrew boys? I can go on and on and on. In the world today, there are men and women who have dared to trust God. Is there any one around you? Locate one and study him/her and see what I mean. I tell you, believing on God removes every sorrow and decorates you. Try it today, and I see God doing something great in your life.

Reasons why you have to believe to win.

Why do we need to believe in Him?

- Believing in God is pleasing to him. Hear this:

  "But without faith (belief) it is impossible to please Him: for he that cometh to God must believe that He is, and that he is a rewarder of them that diligently seek him." (Heb 11:6). So, to obtain the very best from God, believing in Him is not negotiable.

- Believing grants you access to his blessing. Hear this:

   "That if thou shalt confess with thy mouth the Lord Jesus, and shalt believe in thine heart that God hath raised him from the dead, thou shall be saved. For with the heart man believeth unto righteousness..." (Rom 10:9-10). Since salvation is the passport to divine blessings, belief, therefore, grants one access to His blessings.

- Believing removes condemnation. Hear this;

   "He that believeth on Him is not condemned: but he that believeth not is condemned already, because he hath not believed in the name of the only begotten Son of God." (Jn 3:18).

- In the same John, we are told that believing procures everlasting life;

   "He that believeth on the Son hath everlasting life: and he that believeth not the Son shall not see life; but the wrath of God abideth on him." (Jn 3:36).

What then is the meaning of believing?

Having said all these, I will like to define Believing as beginning to live. All this while, you have merely existed. But now you have a choice to start living – live as a child of God, and then you shall be able to meet your needs, decide what comes to you, chose what you want, etc. You cannot afford to miss this golden chance.

Having seen the benefits of believing in the Son of God – Jesus Christ – I trust God that your level of belief will increase that you be not condemned, or face the wrath of God. As you chose to apply this key today to enhance your life, I pray that the issue in your life for which you have suffered so much shame be wiped away, in Jesus excellent name, Amen.

What you must believe.

You may ask me, what am I supposed to believe? The answer is very simple. Believe everything the Bible says concerning you.

Start by believing that Jesus Christ is the Son of God, that He came and died for you and me; that He was raised again from the dead and is now at the right hand of the father interceding for you and me.

Then go on to believe that you are ordained to be a success, not a failure; the head and not the tail, healthy and not sickly, a wonder to your world and not a wonderer, a child of destiny and not a destitute, a child of God and not a slave or servant of God, a child of promise and not a problem.

When you believe all these and much more, you then need the very next vital key to access them. Let me, therefore, introduce you to the passport that will grant you entrance into the kingdom where all these are available, the key of salvation.

CHAPTER SEVEN

SALVATION

"You are not safe until you are saved."

Discovery tells us of our destination in Christ - where we are going to. It allows us to see it. Revelation makes it real to us and shows us how to get there as it provides us with the needed compass. Believing empowers us to take steps and provides the strength and courage to go after the high callings of the LORD. However, salvation is the visa, gate-pass, or passport that allows you to enter this Promised Land. Even if we manage to get to the gate of our inheritance without salvation (which I strongly doubt), access will be denied. Jesus speaking on salvation said,

"Verily, verily, I say unto thee, except a man be born again, he cannot see the Kingdom of God. (Jn 3:3).

Why is salvation necessary?

Why do we need to be born again, change our thoughts, ideas, actions, beliefs, behaviors, manners, language and attitudes? Let me take you on a journey into the Bible.

Once upon a time, God the father convened a very important conference in heaven. The only agenda for the meeting was man. In the conference, God the father said,

"Let us make man in our own image, after our own likeness: and let him have dominion over the fish of the sea, and over the fowl of the air, and over the cattle, and over all the earth, and over every creeping thing that creepeth upon the earth." (Gen 1:26). God created man in His own image, after His likeness and manner to make them the master of everything he created, including Satan. God went further to bless them, and said,

"Be fruitful, and multiply, and replenish the earth, and subdue it: and have dominion over the fish of the sea, and over the fowl of the air, and over every living thing that moveth upon the earth." (Gen 1:28). And God gave them in addition, every herb bearing seed, which is upon the face of all the earth, and every tree, in which is the fruit of a tree yielding seed, every beast of the earth, every fowl of the air, everything that creepeth upon the earth, and everything wherein there is life, for meat. And it was so.

Thus, God made man a god to the circumstances of life, a master over life challenges, and a king over and above the devil. This position was highly exalted that Man had no problem that the answer was not readily available. Before a challenge arose, he already knew what to do. He had the excellent mind of God. As an idle mind is the devil's workshop, God decided to keep man busy. To achieve this, God planted a garden wherein there was everything that pertains to life and put the man into it just "to dress it and to keep it." (Gen 2:15).

In this garden, man had no needs he could not meet, was never designed to be sick, or suffer lack of any kind. He even had the mind of God, the wisdom of the most high, and the capabilities of Christ. This made the devil, the god of this world, to be very angry. He – the devil – knew that if men were allowed to multiply in this elevated position, his authority on earth would be forever taken away from him. So, he became jealous, and started to plot to offset man and to take over his position. He knew God very well, how Holy God is and how much God hates iniquity; and for him (devil) to succeed, he had to make man to sin against God. This he did. He succeeded when man disobeyed God's instructions.

With disobedience, man lost his position of authority, dominion and respect. He also lost God's fellowship. This made fear to come in. God got angry and cursed the earth, the woman and the serpent for man's sake. This curse coupled with the entrance of fear broke the hedge. Man then became a victim of all sorts of life afflictions, problems and challenges.

Several attempts were made to redeem man; animals were killed, sacrifices were offered, but all procured only temporary solutions to the problems of man. The curse was still hanging over all creation. God knew that He had to do something drastic to forever redeem man, so he sent Jesus Christ.

Man was in this deplorable state until the coming of Jesus the Christ. Jesus came to restore man to the lost position, lost glory, lost status, lost dominion and to repair the lost relationship between man and God. It is only those that accept Him that are, therefore, allowed to enjoy this new status in God. That is why today, you need this key called salvation. I, therefore, boldly present to you this fundamental key for kingdom excellence and making maximum impact in life.

What is salvation?

Salvation, to me, simply means, "Salvaging what has been lost." It is God's process of taking back from Satan all he took away from man, and, restoring them back to man.

God made man to be a wonder to the world. Everything was made to answer to him while he answers only to God – his maker. No wonder the Bible said,

"Behold, I and the children whom the LORD hath given me are for signs and for wonders..." (Is 8:18). Salvation is what it takes to restore man back to this wonder status. It is, therefore, your re-initiation into a position of authority, dominion, 'rulership', and back into your Garden of Eden.

Salvation takes you to a position where no earthly challenge can molest you. It takes you to a place that is...

"Far above all principalities, and power, and might, and dominion, and every name that is named, not only in this world, but also in that which is to come:" (Eph 1:21). How do I know this? Because He said in the next chapter concerning all of us that have received Jesus Christ as our Lord and personal saviour, that is, all those that have been saved, that God, "has raised us up together, and made us to sit together in heavenly places in Christ Jesus." (Eph 2:6). These positions are exclusively for those who hath been delivered from the powers of darkness – sin and death – and hath being translated into the kingdom of His dear Son Jesus through salvation.

This means that you have no access to the things of God if you do not make amends with Him. How can you even obtain something from a kingdom you cannot see? Now is the time. Without this step, suffering continues. A life without Christ is a life full of crisis.

Does salvation have any other benefit(s)?

Yes. Let us look at some of these other benefits of salvation.

❖ Salvation changes your life 360^0.

> **"Marvel not that I said unto you, Ye must be born again. The wind bloweth where it listeth, and thou hearest the sound thereof, but canst not tell whence it cometh, and whither it goeth: so is every one that is born of the spirit." (Jhn 3:7-8).** Like the wind which can be felt but not seen, every born-again person – that is every true Christian – is unstoppable, 'unhandleable', 'unmolestable', unchallengeable, unpredictable, and 'unarrestable', but irresistible. They are difficult to analyze, live above failures, successful, and a lot more. You may not be able to explain him, but you cannot deny his results. You may even hate him, but you cannot stop him. You see his results, but you cannot explain them.

❖ Salvation initiates you into a world of wonders. Hear this,

"And all these signs shall follow them that believe, In my name shall they cast out devils; they shall speak with new tongue; they shall take up serpents; and if they drink any deadly thing, it shall not hurt them; they shall lay hands on the sick, and they shall recover." (Mk 16:17- 18). If a life of wonder is what you desire, then salvation is what you need.

❖ Salvation turns you into a new man. Hear the Holy Scriptures,

"Therefore, if any man be in Christ, he is a new creature: old things are passed away; behold, all things are become new." (2 Cor 5:17). New man means a man free of the old baggage and challenges, free of sin, curses, sicknesses and whatever my Father has not planted. A new man!

❖ Salvation gives you a new status. Before you gave your life to Christ, the Bible did not reckon with you as a human being, but once your life is saved, the Bible calls you a member of a chosen generation.

"But ye are a chosen generation, a royal priesthood, an holy nation, a peculiar people; that ye should show forth the praises of Him who hath called you out of darkness into His marvelous light. Which in time past were no people, but are now the people of God:" (2 Pet

2:9-10). In order words, before regeneration that comes with new birth, we had similar status with any animal, but after salvation, our status automatically changed. Salvation makes you very precious to God and the world at large.

❖ Salvation grants you access to the excellent things of God. Without salvation, you cannot even see them; talk less of enjoying or partaking in them. Hear this again,

"Verily, verily, I say unto thee, except a man be born again, he cannot see the kingdom of God." (Jhn 3:3). Except one is saved, one cannot see the blessings of God, which are found only in His kingdom. These blessings include peace, joy, happiness, provisions, protection, long-life, health, fruitfulness, and restoration of lost relationships, lost inheritances, lost resources, lost love life, lost homes, lost promises, etc. This is what the Master Himself said.

To emphasize how important this step is, He reiterated this in verse five of the same chapter, saying that except a man be born again, he cannot enter the kingdom of God. Do you want to enter into God's plans and purposes for your life, are you tired of a wilderness experience, are you weary of doing it your own way with all the confusions and challenges that bring a lot of frustrations, are you totally exhausted by sweating through life without commensurate results to show for your works, and do you want a new lease of life with God as your new partner? Then I am proud to show you the more excellent way. **Jesus Christ is the only answer that lasts.**

What to do.

To be saved, you must believe and be baptized, otherwise you are condemned already. This is not my judgment but God's.

"He that believeth and is baptized shall be saved; but he that believeth not shall be damned." (Mk 16:16). Becoming saved, therefore, requires just two things – believing with your heart and confessing with your mouth. Baptism (both of water and Holy Spirit) are important and helps to fulfill all righteousness as well as empowers you to excel, but they do not save. What saves is this,

"That if thou shalt confess with thy mouth the Lord Jesus, and shalt believe in thine heart that God hath raised him from the dead, thou shall be saved. For with the heart man believeth unto righteousness; and with the mouth confession is made unto salvation." (Rom 10:9-10).

Jesus talking to John just before His baptism in water said,

"Suffer it to be so now: for thus it becometh us to fulfill all righteousness." (Mt 3:15).

And while speaking to His disciples about the baptism of the Holy Spirit, said,

"But ye shall receive power, after the Holy Ghost is come upon you: and ye shall be..." (Acts 1:8).

Embracing Jesus Christ is therefore your number one step in actualizing your nature in God. There are no two ways to it. Jesus is the way, and to use this way, you must be born again. Salvation is your gate-pass on Christ way.

Therefore, if you have not yet given your life to Christ, now is the time. Take time out now to pray this sinners' prayer. And as you do this, I see God welcoming you into His kingdom. You cannot afford to waste more time. This is because you can only boast of now. You cannot, as an unbeliever, be able to say for sure what will happen in the next few seconds. Also, remember that no one comes to Him except the ones that He draws to Himself. He is drawing you now, do not say no to Him. This may be your last chance!

Please do not joke with your destiny and life, make the confession now. Let's pray...

Almighty Father, I come to You just as I am. I know that I cannot save or help myself. I have sinned against You in thoughts, words and deeds. Now, I have made up my mind to forsake my old ways. Forgive me my sins and deliver me from the power of sin and death. Today Lord, I accept You as my Lord and Saviour. Cancel my name from the book of death and accept me into the kingdom of Your dear son, Jesus Christ. Baptize me with the grace to run this new race of life with You. Establish me in Your ways, and turn my weaknesses into strength. Thank You for changing

***and accepting me, and making me a child of God, in Jesus mighty name, Amen**.*

Congratulations, you are now a child of God. Old things are passed away; behold, all things have become new. You are a new creature; your sins are forgiven and your name has just entered into the Lambs book of life. I feel a very strong urge to remind you that this is the most important decision you have ever made in your whole life. And as such, your life can never remain the same. You are now on your way to the tops. Welcome.

However, if after all this my pleading, you still refused to yield your life to Him, then just close this book and return it to where you bought it for a full refund. This is because from now onwards, I shall be speaking only to those who have given their lives to God and are true children of God.

Peradventure you have given your life to God some time ago, but have made some mistakes because of the cares of this world, there is restoration and reconciliation awaiting you right now. I have something unique for you in the very next chapter.

CHAPTER EIGHT

RECONCILIATION

*"Returning back to where you missed it is a
wise step to excellence and impact."*

A good surprise for you.

Maybe you had given your life to Christ some time ago
and you are saying to yourself, *'this is not for me, it is for
the unbelievers'*. Maybe you have been born again for
twenty years or even more, maybe you are the president
and founder of a ministry, maybe your father is the pastor
of the world's largest church, it may even be that you are
an ordained worker in the house of God. All these are
very good, but they are not and never enough. God has a
surprise for you.

Most of the deprivations believers suffer in life are because
they have left God's work for too long – and God is not
happy about it at all. He desires that you come back to Him
now. You maybe a church worker, a unit head, a parish
priest, or a bishop. You may even be saying, *"after all, I
am a church worker, I go to church four times a week, I*

pay my tithe and give my offerings, I love God and work for Him in His sanctuary, etc."

How enthusiastic are you to the things of God. Are you still as committed as you were when you got born again? Or has the zeal waxed cold over the years. Are you still serving God because you love God or so as to please people, or to avoid questions from people? How is your present work with God?

What reconciliation means

Reconciliation in this context is "recalling, restoring, repairing, and remaking a lost relationship; in this case a lost relationship with God". This means that there was a relationship before which was either taken for granted, or destroyed knowingly or unknowingly, which now needs to be reconsidered and repaired.

At salvation, we started a walk with God; that was when the relationship was developed. Any deviation from the route of that walk takes us away from the Master, and today He is asking us to return.

The Bible says,

"Unto the angel of the church of Ephesus write *(please put your name in place of church of Ephesus)...*I know thy works, and thy labour, and thy patience, and how thou canst not bear them which are evil: and thou hast tried them which say they are apostles, and are not, and hast found them liars: And hast borne, and hast patience, and for my name's sake hast laboured, and hast not fainted." (Rev 2:1-3).

This is a wonderful credential for any Christian, especially for you. The King of kings Himself is saying that He knows your works. He opened the book of records and found your name on it. A lot was written concerning your services in the kingdom. He knows your past inputs into the kingdom, your faith that could move mountains, your trust and patience in God, your day by day labour and sacrifices, your fasting, prayers, your enthusiasm for the things of God, your love for God and His kingdom, your extra-ordinary commitments to His works, and your willingness to give as and when due. He knows about how you have favoured the stones of Zion and your love for Him. He said that He knows all these. What a wonderful and reassuring information.

However, this was your status when you just got born again and maybe few days, weeks, months, or even years thereafter. Since then it is like things have changed. You are now comfortable seeing evil, you find it difficult to dedicate your time to the things of God anymore, and you are now very busy because of God's blessings in your life. The family that God gave you and personally protected, provided for, and secured makes it now difficult for you to serve God. Your job, which God gave to you after several prayers of supplications and petitions, and vows to Him now comes before God in your list of priorities. Any simple affliction is a reason to curse God. Your complaints have no end. You even believe that God owes you for your services to the kingdom. And peradventure you are now an ordained worker, you feel that you have arrived, you have achieved your objectives, and everyone should now respect and serve you. God is saying to you now,

"Nevertheless I have something against thee," (Rev 2:4). What does He have against you? It is right there in the second part of the above scripture; "because you have left your first love."

What has God against you? Think about it for a moment. Where have you left God? He went on to say,

"Remember therefore from whence thou art fallen, and repent, and do the first works; or else I will come unto thee quickly, and will remove thy candle-stick out of its place, except thou repent." (Rev 2:5).

Ask yourself...

Where and when have you left your first love? God is requesting you to remember when you left Him, where you departed from Him, and are fallen, and repent. He is asking you now to go back to your first love or face His wrought.

He is saying that if you do not 're-paint' your life with His words – that is, your first love – that he will remove your candlestick – that is, demobilize you, make you ineffective and even take your life away. When God takes away your candlestick, which is the Spirit of the Lord, real trouble begins. He is, therefore, asking you to change your position and make amends.

If, like the men Peter preached to in Acts chapter two, you are pricked in your heart now and is asking "Men and brethren, what shall we do?" (Acts 2:37). I will answer you also in the same manner that Peter answered them by saying, "Repent, and be baptized every one of you in the name of Jesus Christ for the remission of sins, and ye shall receive the gift of the Holy Ghost." (Acts 2:38).

What you must do.

If you want to enjoy God, and the full restoration of all that the devil has stolen from you, you must return to where you missed it, you must restore yourself back to where you used to be, you must repair the cracks that exist between you and God, and remake the bond of fellowship.

Your yesterday's good works are not sufficient for today; neither can they replace your daily commitment to God. Every day must see you drawing nearer to God, so that God too can draw near to you (James 4:8).

Fasting and praying cannot replace your sincere walk with God. If you will be willing and obedient today to return to your exalted position and recall your relationship with Him, your hours of fasting and prayers may greatly reduce.

Do you know that...

The testimony of your walk with God is your greatest evidence in your moment of challenges. If therefore you do not have a good testimony of a walk with God, you are running a risk.

To reconcile us with God was actually the main reason why Christ came. Thus, refusing this ministry of reconciliation is refusing the faith.

"And all things are of God, who hath reconciled us to himself by Jesus Christ, and hath given to us the ministry of reconciliation." (2 Cor 5:18). And thus, "...we were reconciled to God by the death of His Son," (Rom.:5:10).

Do something now.

I know that you know where you stopped, went your own way, derailed from the course and lost your commitment. The Spirit of God is saying to you now, 'go back there.'

Are you living the life of a prodigal son? Return home. The doors are wide open now and always for you if you return. But you do not have the whole time to do this. Now is therefore the accepted time, yes, now is the time of salvation. I say return.

If you left because for sometime now you have been in the faith, yet your expectations were not met, and things seem not to be working, I say unto you,

"Be not deceived; God is not mocked: for whatsoever a man soweth, that shall he also reap." Therefore, "let us not be weary in well doing: for in due season we shall reap, if we faint not." (Gal 6:7,9). If you are yet to receive it then it is not yet late for you, for "no good thing will He withhold from them that walk uprightly." (Ps 84:11).

I therefore ask you to come back, and re-

"Acquaint now thyself with Him, and be at peace: thereby good shall come unto thee. Receive, I pray thee, the law from His mouth, and lay up His words in thine heart." (Job 22:21-22).

The longer you stay far from God, the more you suffer. Learn a lesson from the fig tree called the prodigal son. He had no other name but that of a prodigal son. That will tell you how bad he was. We frequently condemn him for what we were told he did. How many of us will boldly claim that we have not at one time or the other gone the prodigal way? But the errors you committed in ignorance; God overlooked. Now He is asking you to return to base.

As long as the prodigal son was outside, anything was allowed to happen to him. The same is the situation of many Christians today. As long as you are outside the security network of God, Satan is free to feed on you. Maybe like the prodigal son you are afraid to come back home, not knowing the kind of reception that awaits you. Try and also do what he did. Encourage yourself and return home, and like the case of the prodigal son, who "when he was yet a great way off, his father saw him and had compassion, and ran, and fell on his neck, and kissed him." I see God doing much more for you.

In addition, as his father commanded and changed his raiment with kingly robe, killed a fatted calf for him and had a great party in his honour, I see our great and loving God marking your return with enviable blessing that will make your enemies and friends to wonder at you. But please, return.

Do you know why your return is a must?

Without a total return, you can do nothing. Hear the master Himself,

"As the branch cannot bear fruit of itself, except it abide in the vine; no more can ye, except ye abide in me. I am the vine, ye are the branches: He that abideth in me, and I in him, the same bringeth forth much fruit: for without me ye can do nothing. If a man abide not in me, he is cast forth as a branch, and is withered;" (Jn 15:4-6). You see, your only hope of making it is in your returning. You may be asking, 'wherein shall I return?' Let me answer you by asking you my own questions too.

Where are those long hours you used to stay with God in prayer and supplications, that enthusiasm that made you always willing to work for God, and share the word even in buses? What happened to your commitment to your service group where you used to be the most active, your promptness in obeying God and committing your resources to the expansion of the kingdom? The list is quite endless.

Do yourself a favour. Return now. And as you return, I prophesy total restoration of the years and substances you have lost.

May God give you the grace to return and be reconciled to your redeemer, for a brighter future, Amen.

Now that you have fully reconciled with God, you are ready for kingdom excellence and maximum impact in life and ministry. This is an exclusive preserve of those who are in the good book of God. Welcome to your season of smiles and jubilation.

PART THREE

ENHANCING KEYS

"Nobody rents a foundation; No matter how beautiful it looks."

The fact that you are reading this section means that you are a bona-fide, legitimate, and authentic child of God, and have completely reconciled your ways with Him. I sincerely congratulate you for your current status with God. You shall never regret signing in for Him.

Having laid a very solid foundation in Part two, there is a great need for us to build on it for your excellence to be made manifest to all. In this section, we will be discussing some vital keys that will enhance your walk with God. These, I have chosen to call enhancing keys.

The result you will obtain from now onwards will greatly depend on the kind of foundation you laid for yourself and the proper application of these keys. Remember the nature of the foundation determines how high and how strong the building will be. I will take it that you did lay a solid foundation for yourself; having willingly given your life to Christ or reconciled yourself back to your first love and first works based on knowledge.

Nobody however, lives in a foundation, neither do people rent foundations as homes of residence. No matter how beautiful a foundation may be, nobody moves into it for habitation. To this end, foundations are only useful if a befitting structure is erected on them. These enhancing keys will help you erect a befitting structure on your solid and firm foundation.

Remember, "every house is builded by some man: but he that built all things is God."(Heb 3:4). You have a duty to build your own spiritual house based on the scriptures – praying for divine assistance and support to take the right and best steps per time. I believe God that He will use this section to enhance your ability, reduce sweating and struggles, and increase results.

Ecclesiastes 10:15 said, "The labour of the foolish wearieth everyone of them, because he knoweth not how to go to the city." Attempting to build on a foundation without wisdom is very frustrating. These keys, which are wisdom buttons, shall make your labour not only fruitful and rewarding, but also very interesting. For, "except the Lord build a house, they labour in vain that build it:"(Ps 127:1).No more shall you sweat and have sleepless nights over these issues as God will take over your building for you as you walk in knowledge and wisdom.

So, allow God Himself to build this house for you through these wisdom keys. As you go on reading and applying these wisdom keys, I prophesy total deliverance from all frustrations of life, completion of every uncompleted project, and motion into every stagnated project in any sphere of your endeavor.

CHAPTER NINE

CONFESSION

"Until you confess it, you cannot command it."

'Until you say it, you cannot see it' is a very common saying in the kingdom today. And this is true. When your mouth is closed, your heavens are sealed; and if you fail to confess it, your seeds will not germinate. Life is a product of your confession.

The mouth is a weapon of authority to keep you in perfect dominion. Even in the secular world, it is only a command from the mouth that soldiers obey. Every sign and wonder in the kingdom is a product of a sound. A soundless Christian is a sign-less Christian.

Imagine what the world will have been like if God had decided to keep quiet. Even the word of God has no power to perform on its own until it is given a voice. It is only when it is sent that it can heal any situation and delivers anyone from all forms of destructions. Thus, the Bible said,

"He sent His word, and healed them, and delivered them from their destructions" (Ps.: 107:20).

The Holy Spirit is the voice of the word of God. The entrance of the word sent, giveth light to every issue of life. Outside the word, therefore, total darkness is the order of the day.

Our God is not a dumb God.

To set an example for the world on the need to give a voice to the word and to regularly send it for signs and wonders, God the father created the world through the instrumentality of the word.

The Bible recorded that in the beginning, God created the heaven and the earth. However, the earth was without form and void, and darkness was upon the face of the deep. There was no beauty, no life, no light, and no organization, despite the spirit of God that moved upon the face of the waters. Everything was just disorganized. There was confusion, chaos, disorder and disarray everywhere.

To bring order to this order-less situation, God had no choice but to speak. "Let there be light:" This simple statement started a chain of activities. Immediately God said that, there was light. God saw that it was good, and divided the light from the darkness, calling the light day and the darkness night. This great success inspired God to go on with other aspects of creation. God had to keep speaking to see what He wanted.

The rules have not changed – what you say determines what you see. If you also want to see anything good, you must have to speak – saying what you want so that you may see what you desire. Remember, if you say what you do not want, you will have what you do not want. So be careful with your mouth for the Bible says that a man shall eat good by the fruits of his mouth (Prov 13:2).

Speak, speak and speak.

Maybe, like the earth before God spoke, your life is without form and void, in total disarray; confusion, panic, uncertainty, dismay and alarm; maybe darkness – spiritual and or physical darkness – is all over your life, and you are at a loss as to what to do. Do what God did, and you will see what He saw. And as you speak, that emptiness shall be converted into fullness, the darkness shall be turned into light and the void shall be destroyed and everything shall be put into shape.

Do you know why? Because He spoke and saw good, if you too shall speak in accordance with His word, you too shall see good.

As God kept on saying, He kept on seeing. There is therefore no limit to what you have to say. As long as there is life in you, do not stop speaking and you will not stop seeing.

Jesus also was not a dumb Christ. He spoke everywhere He went, just like the father. And as He opened His mouth, signs and wonders always followed. Knowing therefore the power in spoken words, He advised all Christians, saying,

"Have faith in God. For verily I say unto you, That whosoever shall say unto this mountain, Be thou removed, and be thou cast into the sea; and shall not doubt in his heart, but shall believe that those things which he saith shall come to pass; he shall have whatsoever he saith." (Mk 11:23-23).

The journey to obtaining results starts with faith – having faith in God. When your faith is certified, then you must speak the word, believing that what you said is possible, and the Bible said that you must surely obtain what you said.

The mountain before you now may be sickness, poverty, barrenness, joblessness, advancing age without a life partner, generational curses, stagnation, frustration, depression, difficult spouse, troublesome children, etc. Whatever the mountain maybe, the Bible said if and only if you will say what you want concerning it, with total belief, that you will have whatever you desire.

Are you willing to face these mountains before you now? If you are, then go on and declare what you want, and I see our ever-faithful father granting you what you have just said.

When God wanted to create man, hear Him,

"And God said, Let us make man in our own image, after our likeness: and let them have…So God created man in His own image, in the image of God created He him; male and female created He them." (Gen.: 1:26-27).

God could have just bent down and started molding man from the dust of the earth. But He didn't. Rather He first declared what He wanted before bending down to create. This put His desire in proper perspective, and also brought out the creative ability and power of God.

Secondly, we were made in God's image, and, therefore, have the same spirit of faith; we must therefore speak as He did, to create our own expected and dream world. Until we speak, nothing speaks in our life.

"We having the same spirit of faith, according as it is written, I believed, and therefore have I spoken; we also believe, and therefore speak." (2 Cor 4:13). Therefore, to create a dream world, speak, speak and speak His word.

This is the only true evidence of belief – confession. Do you know that without confession, our belief is questionable? Because he who believes, must as a necessity confess what he believes in – calling forth those things that be not as though they were. (Rom 4:17).

Why you must speak.

Anybody can say what he or she likes about you. But what are you saying about yourself? What opinion do you have about your future? Whose report are you willing to believe?

It is actually what you say that will come to pass in your life. However, when you seal your mouth, what they say may come to pass. Why? Because the angels that excel in strength are the reapers of our harvest, and they obey the word (Ps.: 103:20). So, if they are dormant for a long time, they may start obeying the orders of your enemies. To avoid this from happening, speak, speak and keep on speaking.

Do you know that what you are seeing today is what you said yesterday (knowingly or unknowingly), and what you say today is what will shape, produce and deliver what you shall see tomorrow? Bold declarations provoke the miraculous. This is because the words that we speak are spirit and they are life. Jesus even said it Himself,

"It is the spirit that quickeneth; the flesh profiteth nothing: the words that I speak unto you, they are spirit, and they are life." (Jn 6:63).

And because they are spirit, they are able to invade the spirit realm to bring unto us all our blessings which are stockpiled in the spirit world. Do not forget that everything we see today is obtained from things unseen.

"Through faith we understand that the worlds were framed by the word of God, so that things which are seen were not made of things which do appear." (Heb 11:3). In order words, things which we see today, were framed from unseen things. Looking at the book of Genesis Chapter One, this statement becomes so real.

Don't keep the word to yourself. Speak it.

Speak, but speak right.

However, telling you to speak does not mean that anything that gets into your mind you shall speak. No. You are allowed to speak only the word of faith for kingdom exploits. Any other word can destroy your life. Hear this,

"But what saith it? The word is nigh thee, even in thy mouth, and in thy heart: that is, the word of faith, which we preach." (Rom 10:8). You see, the word of faith, which is what you ought to speak continually is near thee – actually right there in your mouth – speak it, therefore, that both you and your children may be justified. Speaking any other word may be suicidal. Remember,

"Death and life are in the power of the tongue: and they that love it shall eat the fruit thereof." (Prov 18:21).

When you speak the word of God, which is the word of faith, you have life and have it more abundantly; however, if you chose to speak the counsel of the enemy, you will have death, destruction and loses.

As you choose today to speak and to speak well, your heavens will finally open up for you. Nobody is well enough to kill you, stop your progress or afflict you with illness.

You are the worse enemy of yourself. Do not hinder your progress yourself by not declaring your desires. Start now, start today, and the sky shall be your starting point.

Always check yourself.

You may be asking me now, 'how do I know when I am speaking well?' You will know if you are a child of God by the witness of the spirit. Ask yourself always, what is the Bible saying about this situation, what is the Bible saying about me, how did my covenant fathers overcome similar challenges etc.? When you discover what the book of life has said concerning the situation, then declare it.

God sees you as the head and not the tail, the first and not the last, above only and never beneath. How do you see yourself? God said,

"For I know the thoughts that I think towards you, saith the Lord, thoughts of peace and not of evil, to give you an expected end (*that is, a future and a hope*)." (Jer 29:11).

"For since the beginning of the world men have not heard, nor perceived by the ear, neither hath eye seen, O God, beside thee, what he hath prepared for him that waiteth for him." (Is 64:4). To emphasize this prophecy, Paul used it in this way,

"Eye hath not seen, nor ear heard, neither have entered into the heart of man, the things which God hath prepared for them that love Him." (1 Cor 2:9). Do you love God? Then see yourself as one of those God has chosen to justify and glorify.

Therefore, speak always His words, not your words. Another reason why you must speak His words only is because He alone sees your tomorrow; He always knows the end from the beginning. Isaiah testifying to this said,

"Declaring the end from the beginning, and from the ancient times the things that are not yet done, saying, My counsel shall stand, and I will do all my pleasure:" (Is 46:10). He alone knows what He has prepared for you, and where He is taking you. Above all, His thoughts are far higher than your thoughts,

"For my thoughts are not your thoughts, neither are your ways my ways, saith the Lord. For as the heavens are higher than the earth, so are my ways higher than your ways, and my thoughts than your thoughts." And any word that proceeds from His mouth, "shall not return unto me void, but it shall accomplish that which I please, and it shall prosper in the thing whereto I sent it." (Is 55:8-11). Thus, speak only His words and thoughts for He has better and higher thoughts and plans. Trust Him enough to commit all your ways to Him. I promise you, He will never fail you. Furthermore, God is only committed to confirming and fulfilling His words.

Do you not know...

That the words that we speak do to our destiny what water does to our plantings. Imagine planting some precious gardens and forgetting or refusing to water it, especially in the dry season. All the seeds planted will be lost. And no harvest will be seen. Thus, Paul wrote,

"I have planted, Apollos watered; but God gave the increase." (1 Cor 3:6). God always waits for our watering before giving the increase. Be ye not slothful in well doing. Plan to and actually water your seed, and your harvest will be the envy of the world. Remember Isaac, he planted, watered, and in the same year reaped a hundred-fold return (Gen 26:1,12-15,19-22). And "we, brethren, as Isaac was, are the children of promise." (Gal 4:28). So, let us do what he did that we may become what he became. Water your seeds.

Furthermore, nobody waters his plantings with acid or toxic chemicals. Bad language is like acid to our destiny. So, speak right words always. Speak the word!

These are good examples.

Let me show you some people that made it in the Bible by saying what they wanted. I have already reminded you of the story of creation by God, the Father. Please read Genesis Chapter One again.

Abraham was also a man that spoke and got what he wanted. Remember his encounter with the Angels enroute Sodom and Gomorrah. He stopped them, requested that they be refreshed in his home, and then requested for the life of Lot and his family. He got all. Confirm what I am saying in Genesis Chapter 18:1-end, and 19:1-22.

Moses was another man that obtained what he wanted by speaking his mind. This was despite the fact that God had made him a god to Pharaoh (Ex. 7:1). To show Pharaoh that he was truly a god, Moses spoke most times through Aaron; but whenever he was about to request anything from the Lord, he spoke to God himself. Also, whenever he was about to manifest the power of God, he spoke himself – just to show that life is a product of personal adventures and encounters. In one of such occasions, he said,

"Fear ye not, stand still, and see the salvation of the Lord, which he will show to you today: for the Egyptians whom ye have seen today, ye shall see them no more forever. The Lord shall fight for you, and ye shall hold your peace." (Ex 14:13-14). Watch his statement. He was declaring what he wanted God to do for them. God was yet to speak and direct him on how to overcome the challenge in the subsequent verses. But he was so sure that God will definitely save them that he started declaring what he wanted before hearing from God, and God was faithful. He always backs whatever we say in faith. If only you can trust God enough, you will obtain similar testimonies.

Sometime later, the children of Israel were once more faced with a great challenge.

"Now Jericho was straitly shut up because of the children of Israel: none went out, and none came in." (Jos 6:1). Hunger would have killed them if they had not decided to do something. The marching round of Jericho could not fall the wall. Only a shout – bold declaration – could.

Today as you decide to speak out, every Egyptian you see today, you shall see no more forever, and all walls standing between you and your promised land shall fall flat. As you invite God into that issue of yours today, by speaking His words back to Him, I see Him fight for you, while you hold your peace, in the mighty name of Jesus, Amen.

Result producing confessions.

For your words to produce result after the manner of Moses, Jesus, Peter, and Paul, it must be:

- Faith filled. For "without faith, it is impossible to please Him:" (Heb 11:6)
- Spirit filled. Jesus said, "The words that I speak unto you, they are spirit, and they are life." (Jn 6:63). Follow therefore His footsteps, and you will obtain results after His kind.
- Spoken with authority, and forcefully. Speak as one with authority. Remember the centurion who said,

"I am a man under authority, having soldiers under me: and I say to this man, Go, and he goeth; and to another, Come, and he cometh; and to my servant, Do this, and he doeth it." (Mt 8:8-9). Like him, there are several spiritual forces working under you. You need words spoken with authority to move them to work. Also, the enemies you are dealing with do not hear soft words. You cannot cajole them out. You must manifest your authority for them to move. So, use your position as God's ambassador and put all your enemies to flight.

- Spoken at the right time, for "How forcible are right words!" (Job 6:25). Speak only in due time. Don't waste your words. Use them as and when due.

Results of right words.

When words are correctly applied, miracles are born. The woman with the issue of blood said in her heart, "If I may but touch his garment, I shall be whole." (Mt 9:21). So, whether you say it out or not, it does not matter. Just say it right, and miracle will be born.

No matter how bad the situation may look, there is no closed case with God. For with Him, all things are possible.

Moreover, words – which serve as water – can bring back to life what seemed dead. If only you can believe no matter what the situation is, there is always hope. Look at this report in Job;

"For there is hope of a tree, if it be cut down, that it will sprout again, and that the tender branch thereof will not cease. *(How?).* Though the root thereof wax old in the earth, and the stock thereof die in the ground; yet through the scent of water *(delivered by words)* it will bud, and bring forth boughs like a plant *(that is be fruitful).*" (Job 14:7-9).

This is what the spoken word could do. I therefore deliver this key to you today. Use it and excel. See you at the top.

CHAPTER TEN

POSITIVE THINKING

"You are what you think! Think right, and live right"

The benefits of positive thinking have been the subjects of many years of discussions. However, positive thinking in the kingdom is relatively new.

By positive thinking, I do not mean believing that your thought can save you. No. It is very important for me to make this clarification from the start to avoid any misconceptions that may arise.

What then is positive thinking?

What I mean by positive thinking is *'thinking only on the promises of God for your life, believing that they are certain and real, and that with God on your side, they will never fail.'* Positive thinking in the kingdom is equivalent to obeying totally the Biblical injunction as contained in the book of Philippians,

"Finally, brethren, whatsoever things are true, whatsoever things are honest, whatsoever things are just, whatsoever things are pure, whatsoever things are lovely, whatsoever things are of good report; if there be any virtue, and if there be any praise, think on these things. (Phil 4:8).

Your thoughts are important too.

Your thought is a major key to kingdom excellence. That is why what you think about matters a lot. No wonder the Bible warned us, saying

"Keep thy heart with all diligence; for out of it are the issues of life. (Prov 4:23). To buttress the fact that our thought makes or mars our lives, the same Proverbs stated,

"For as he thinketh in his heart, so is he(Prov 23:7). If therefore we desire a smooth, problem free, poverty absent, overcomer's life, we then must think always in the right perspective. There is no other way out.

Many peoples' lives today are laden with all manners of problems just because they brought it upon themselves by their thoughts. Just as God is committed to bringing to pass everything you declare with your mouth – whether good or bad – so also is He committed to your thoughts – whether positive or negative.

For He is able to do exceedingly above all you think and ask. At least that is what Apostle Paul said,

"Now unto Him that is able to do exceedingly abundantly above all that we ask or think, according to the power that worketh in us," (Eph 3:20). So, to see only positive things in the kingdom, think positive always.

Why think right?

With God, there is never a closed case. Some situations may look so hopeless, but if we remember that God cannot refer our case to any other person and that he is able to do all things, then it becomes a lot easier to think positively concerning that situation or issue. Jesus said to a man whose child was possessed by demon, which His disciples could not help, "If thou canst believe, all things are possible to him that believeth." (Mk 9:23). In other words, 'if thou can think it through in your mind, and accept it in your heart that your son can be well again, and recognize that I – the Lord of the whole earth – can do it, then it shall happen right now'.

This is exactly what He is still saying to us today. Believe in me, and based on your faith in me, think positively in all things. And peradventure a different thought is coming into your mind that will not glorify me, cast it down,

"For the weapons of our warfare are not carnal, but mighty through God to the pulling down of strong holds; Casting down imaginations, and every high thing that exalteth itself against the knowledge of God, and bringing into captivity every thought to the obedience of Christ; and having in a readiness to revenge all disobedience, when your obedience is fulfilled." (2 Cor 10:4-6). Thus, every thought must be brought to the obedience of Christ. Anyone that is contrary to what Christ stands for must be cast down. This, the Bible said, is obedience. As you chose to obey God by thinking like Christ always, I see every disobedience against you being avenged.

There is another reason why you have to think God's thoughts only and always. His thoughts towards you are "thoughts of peace and not of evil, to give you an expected end." (Jer 29:11). If His thoughts towards you are only of peace and designed to bring you into your destiny, then basing all your thoughts in him is a very wise step to take.

You are not the first.

Let me take you down the memory lane to bring to your remembrance some of our covenant fathers that applied this vital key to achieve kingdom excellence. Let us start with Abraham. You know the story of this man very well, so I will not bore you with the details. But imagine yourself changing your name when you are yet barren to answer "the father of many nations"; telling anyone that cared to listen that by you all the nations of the earth shall be blessed; telling your wife who was close to ninety years that she is not barren and thus cause her to change her name to Sarah; and later, reminding everyone what you told them some twenty years earlier when there was no evidence or any physical indication that it will come to pass. But he did all these, and today it has come to pass. He is not only the father of the descendants of Isaac, but also the father of all believers all over the world. What a perfect example of positive thinking.

Do you remember David and Goliath in 1 Samuel 17? Goliath had come believing that he would win and insult the king and God of Israel. He had already started raining down the insults on them. Everyone was afraid of him including the king himself – Saul. The situation was set to

85

end in shame for the children of Israel. It was a dead end so to say. Then came David, a small shepherd boy.

In the circumstance, he saw a chance to launch himself into the world. Every other person saw a problem, but this young wild boy saw an opportunity, a chance to make a mark. They saw a stumbling block, but David saw a stepping-stone. He must have said to himself, "if I can only face this man, I know I will destroy him; however even if I fail to destroy him, it will be on record that I was the only one who had the courage to face him".

Then he recognized Goliath's weak point – Goliath was insulting the living God. So, he thought within himself, 'God cannot allow this uncircumcised Philistine to defile His name', so he said again within himself, 'God will surely do it, not for me, but for His name's sake'. Then God reminded him of how he destroyed a bear and a lion in the forest. His faith was electrified. His thought and bold declarations based on the long hours of positive thinking brought God into the scene. How did it end? David became the toast of the town from that day. He killed Goliath.

Many people that day, including Saul, magnified the problem, but David magnified his God above the problem. No wonder God Himself said concerning David,

"I have found David my servant; with my holy oil have I anointed him: with whom my hand shall be established: mine arm also shall strengthen him. The enemy *(including Goliath)* shall not exact upon him; nor the sons of wickedness afflict him. But my faithfulness and my mercy shall be with him: and in my name *(which he protected from being defiled)* shall his horn be exalted." (Ps 89:20-24). As you chose to trust God and to think what he thinks and say what He says, I see Him also boasting about you like He did with David.

Solomon was not the right person to be chosen to rule in place of his father David; but he was somehow chosen and so became the king. David watched him for a while, defending him before the elders and the true born of the family. But one day David must die and then what?

Solomon recognized that he couldn't rule on his power or wisdom, so he began to think. He remembered what his father told him that God is a God of covenants, and His covenant, He will never break. Fully persuaded, he went to God with an overwhelming sacrifice. His sacrifice moved God and God came down and gave him an open cheque. He got wisdom, riches and fame. Above all, all his enemies respected him, and he had peace on all sides round about him. (1 Kg 4:24).

Again, like his father, positive thinking saw him through. Some people may have dwelled on the problems, the enemies, the challenges, and the angry/annoyed brothers; but he dwelt on how to overcome. He centered his thoughts only on the God his father served faithfully and how he can bring the same God to his side.

Today, as your thoughts center on God, rather than the problem, all your mountains shall be made plain grounds, and all valleys shall be filled up.

There is another man in the Bible whose name was Jabez. Jabez's case was very pathetic. His problem started at birth. His life was a sorrowful one and everything was working against him. Even his mother was against him. For a long time, he allowed it to be. His case was another seemingly closed case. But then, he began to think, 'There must be a way out of this, there must be a way out, God, show me the way.' He refused to focus on the disadvantages, but on God. Then he stumbled on the key of prayer. Over the years he had decided what he wanted, so at the time of prayer, it was not difficult for him to say,

"Oh that thou wouldest bless me indeed, and enlarge my coast, and that thine hand might be with me, and that thou wouldest keep me from evil, that it may not grieve me!" (1 Chron 4:10). And God, our ever-faithful father, granted him that which he requested, and he became more honourable than his brethren.

Your case may not be as bad as that of Jabez, but if you will choose to make God your focus, God will make you a focus on the earth; and every item of shame in your life shall be wiped away.

Hezekiah was also another interesting person in the Old Testament, who refused to think what the situation wanted him to think, but to think positively despite the deadly verdicts. The Bible said that he was sick onto death; and to make matters worse, Isaiah, a great prophet, came and told him to set his house in order, for he shall surely die. Another closed case you may say, but not with this positive thinking man. He remembered what the Bible said concerning him "I shall not die, but live, and declare the works of the Lord." (Ps 118:17). Then he said to God, "the grave cannot praise thee, death cannot celebrate thee… the living, the living, he shall praise thee, as I do this day:" (Is 38:18-19).

Having prayed these prayers, his eyes were opened, and he said to himself, 'I shall not die but live to declare the works of God.' Based on this belief, he never gave up, but kept reminding God of His words. What then happened?

The Bible recorded that God, upon hearing his prayer sent Isaiah back to him. Upon arrival, Isaiah told him that God said,

"I have heard thy prayer, I have seen thy tears: behold, I will add unto thy days fifteen years." (Is 38:5). Every one that is foolish enough to trust on God is never disappointed, and as you make His word your thought book, He will make you a reference point in all the earth.

Let me give you one more example of somebody that applied this principle in her situation and what her rewards were. Remember the woman with the issue of blood? For several years she suffered several things in the hands of so many people, including physicians. She was a subject of ridicule, a reproach to womanhood, a shame to her people, an outcast, somebody everybody saw, but none ever admired or envied, a joke and a wonderer.

She was so frustrated that the roadside became her permanent residence. She was tired of looking for help from anyone having spent all her life possessions in search of cure. She had almost given up hope until she saw Jesus. Then she put on her thinking cap. She said to herself, 'this man has cured the blind, the possessed, the sick, the leper and even raised someone who was dead back to life. My case cannot be that bad that He cannot handle it? He is my only hope; I must go to Him. Even though there is no record of Him curing anyone with my kind of problem, I will still go to Him. Who knows, He may be the solution carrier I have been looking for. Today, I must do something. I will not allow this day to pass me by. After all what have I got to lose.' Having this at the back of her mind therefore, and knowing that people would not allow her to come to Jesus openly to make her request, she said within herself,

"If I may but touch his garment, I shall be whole." (Mt 9:21).

Despising the shame, insults, mockeries, and even molestations from the crowd and apostles, she reached out, pushed through the crowd, and fought the oppositions until she was able to touch the Master. She knew what she was after, so she never gave up until she touched Him. And immediately, she was made whole. What a woman!

Your life is, therefore, a product of your thought life. The more positive you think, the more positive things you see. No matter how dead or impossible the case may look, see it from the eye of God. What is God saying about it? Has anybody in the Bible ever passed through the same road before? If yes, what did the person do to overcome?

And as you take steps to always think like God – believing that all things are possible – I see all obstacles on your way to excellence becoming stepping-stones to your high places in life.

And as you think positively, confess the same, believing totally in it. Remember, it is what you say that you see.

CHAPTER ELEVEN

THE FRUIT OF THE SPIRIT

"Holy Spirit, sweet Holy Spirit; The
power of performance."

**"...But the fruit of the Spirit is love, joy, peace,
longsuffering, gentleness, goodness, faith, meekness,
temperance: against such there is no law." (Gal
5:19-23).**

In the next few chapters, I will be discussing this fruit
as one major key for kingdom excellence and making
maximum impact in life.

The fruit has several components. These are love, joy,
peace, longsuffering, gentleness, goodness, faith,
meekness, and temperance. They are all vital for the
full manifestation of this key. Without any one of these
components, the fruit is incomplete. Therefore, applying
only one of the components is never enough.

What makes a soup is the presence of all the required
ingredients in their right proportions. So, having one or
few of the components of this vital fruit is never enough.

You can see for yourself that the Bible said 'fruit' and not 'fruits', as many people wrongly read and believe. All components of the fruit go hand in hand to procure kingdom excellence.

Look at the above passage again. What do you notice? The Bible said fruit, not gift(s). So, like every other fruit, it can only be obtained from a mature tree – and in this case a mature Spirit. It is never given. To have it, you are always required to do something to produce this fruit.

After the baptism of the Spirit therefore, you are required to nurture, water and protect the Spirit to maturity and tend it until the fruit starts appearing. Even when the fruit starts to appear, you are expected to take care of the Spirit until the fruit is ripe for harvesting.

You have a duty, therefore, to cultivate the Spirit and help it bud, mature, flower, fruit and ripe. Even when it is ripe, you must harvest at the right time, otherwise you may lose your fruits to birds of the air, over-ripeness, and other adversaries. This you must do in and out of season, otherwise the seed will wither away and die.

The Bible further said that outside of this fruit there is no law. Imagine what the world will look like in the absence of love, joy, peace, tolerance, etc. It is as serious as that.

You must therefore, if you desire kingdom excellence, covet this very important fruit, and do everything possible to grow and nurture it to maturity. No effort put into this work is too much.

Now let us take the components one by one and see how they apply to us as believers and their importance. In this chapter, I will be discussing only the first component, that is love. The other components shall be discussed in subsequent chapters.

LOVE

"In the presence of love there are miracles"

Love is the very first component mentioned in our study verse. This is neither a coincidence nor a mistake. It is pre-planned, pre-ordained and allowed for a major purpose. The reason is very simple. Of all the components of the fruit; love is the most important, it is the greatest.

"But covet earnestly the best gifts: and yet show I unto you a more excellent way. Though I speak with the tongues of men and of angels, and have not charity (love), I am become as sounding brass, or a tinkling cymbal. And though I have the gift of prophecy, and understand all mysteries, and all knowledge; and though I have all faith, so that I could remove mountains, and have not love, I am nothing. And though I bestow all my goods to feed the poor, and though I give my body to be burned, and have not love, it profiteth me nothing...And now abideth faith, hope, charity, these three; but the greatest of these is charity (love)" (1 Cor 12:31-13:3, 13).

In this passage, usually referred to as the Chapter of love, we are told that love is the basis of all kingdom gains and achievement. Without love therefore, life is empty, non-profiting and full of frustrations, regrets and misfortunes.

The way of love, the Bible said, is the more excellent way. Thus, it is a vital key towards kingdom excellence and maximum impact in life. Other parts are important, but love is more important.

To let you understand how important love is, the writer went on to say; "And now abideth faith, hope, love, these three; but the greatest of these is love." Why is love the greatest? This is because, in love, you find the other attributes.

What is love?

Love is not a feeling, it is not an emotion, and it is not an affair between two or more people. Love is denying oneself of something important for the sake of others or another person. Love is a price you pay for those you love. It is a sacrifice. Love is thinking, acting and speaking like God, for

"He that loveth not knoweth not God; for God is love". (1 Jn 4:8).

Love is not a confession, it is a way of life; it is giving, sharing and caring so that someone may have a better life, as God Himself did.

"Herein is love, not that we loved God, but that He loved us, and sent His Son to be the propitiation for our sins." (1 Jn 4:10).

"For God so loved the world that he gave His only begotten Son, that whosoever believeth in Him should not perish, but have everlasting life. (Jn 3:16).

Love gives; selfishness takes. Love attracts God; selfishness repels.

Why love?

- If we need to make maximum impact in life, which can only come from divine presence, then we ought to love one another and each other,

"Beloved, if God so loved us, we ought to love one another. No man hath seen God at any time. If we love one another, God dwelleth in us, and His love is perfected in us. God is love; and he that dwelleth in love dwelleth in God, and God in him." (1 Jn 4:11-12, 16).

- Love is the easiest means of attracting and keeping God on our side. For love in us makes our bodies God's dwelling place. And when God dwells in your life, making maximum impact in life becomes a very simple thing, for He will come with all that heaven enjoys and beautify your life.
- True love is not a one-time thing, neither is it a passing moment, for

"Love is as strong as death.... Many waters cannot quench love, neither can the floods drown it." (Song 8:6-7).

- You need light to excel. Light is very necessary for movement and for speed. Without light, speed of accomplishment is reduced, and stumbling is inevitable. Love brings light.

"He that saith he is in the light, and hateth his brother, is in darkness even until now. He

that loveth his brother abideth in the light, and there is none occasion of stumbling in him. But he that hateth his brother is in darkness, and walketh in darkness, and knoweth not whither he goeth, because the darkness hath blinded his eyes." (1 Jn 2:9-11).

- You need love to live, and you need to be alive to excel. A dead man cannot make maximum impact. That is exactly what anyone who does not have love is – a dead man;

"We know that we have passed from death unto life, because we love the brethren. He that loveth not his brother abideth in death." (1 Jn 3:14).

- What is more, the Bible calls anyone who loves not a murderer, and God has absolutely nothing to do with murderers.

"Whosoever hateth his brother is a murderer: and ye know that no murderer hath eternal life abiding in him." (1 Jn 3:15).

Thus, love brings God down to you, makes you eligible for divine helps and confers on you the seal of eternal life.

Some people had used this key.

This was one of the strong keys of David. He loved the Lord and the people. Remember his love for Jonathan, Saul's son. Thus, he could say boldly,

"I will love thee, O LORD, my strength. The LORD is my rock, and my fortress, and my deliverer; my God, my strength, in whom I will trust; my buckler, and the horn of my salvation, and my high tower. I will call upon the LORD...so shall I be saved from my enemies." (Ps 18:1-3).

Because his love for God was certified, God became a defense to him; and always came to his aid anytime he called for assistance.

As your love for the Master today begins to grow and increase, God shall forever be a defense to you and your family. One is not therefore surprised that David became the envy of his generation. The same can happen to you today, as you make up your mind to love God.

Do you know what the Lord said? God said that eye has not seen, nor ear heard, neither has it entered into the heart of man, what he has prepared for those that love Him (1 Cor 2:9). Not for everybody, but just for those that love Him. Do you want to be included in this special list? Then love God. Until your love for God is proven, you are not a candidate for excellence and maximum impacts.

How do I know that you love God?

Simple. You cannot love God unless you love your neighbour who you see and who is always around you. Hear what John said,

"We love Him, because He first loved us. If a man says, I love God, and hateth his brother, he is a liar: for he that loveth not his brother whom he hath seen, how can he love God whom he hath not seen?" (1 Jn 4:19-20).

To emphasize the need to love one another, Jesus said on several occasions, especially when He was asked questions on the greatest commandment,

"Thou shalt love the Lord thy God with all thy heart, and with all thy soul, and with all thy mind. This is the first and great commandment. And the second is like unto it, Thou shalt love thy neighbour as thyself. On these two commandments hang all the law and the prophets. (Mt 22:37-40). To emphasize what He meant by 'on these two commandments hang all the law and the prophets, Mark's gospel recorded it this way,

"There is no other commandment greater than these." (Mk 12:31).

To make you take these sayings of God seriously and live by it, John referred to them as completely new commandments. He quoted Jesus as saying,

"A new commandment I give unto you, that ye love one another; as I have loved you, that ye also love one another. By this shall all men know that ye are my disciples, if ye have love one to another." (Jn 13:34-35).

Being a commandment therefore, Paul called it a debt we owe every man for our salvation to be complete. Hear him,

"Owe no man anything, but to love one another: for he that loveth another hath fulfilled the law." (Rom 13:8). Even in Galatians, he made it clearer by saying,

"For all the law is fulfilled in one word, even in this; Thou shalt love thy neighbour as thyself." (Gal 5:14).

Are you surprised that loving one another is said to be a debt you owe as well as the fulfillment of the laws? Jesus Himself said that there is no other law apart from this one – to love God and your neighbour. So obedience to this law is a passport to heaven, a key to kingdom excellence.

Who is your neighbour? To answer this question, I will like you to spend some time reading the story of the good Samaritan in Luke 10:25-37. I will like to say that you have a duty not only to love those that love you, but much more importantly to love those that hate you. Jesus said,

"Ye have heard that it hath been said, Thou shalt love thy neighbour, and hate thine enemy. But I say unto you, Love your enemies, bless them that curse you, do good to them that hate you, and pray for them which despitefully use you, and persecute you;" (Mt 5:43-44). Why do we have to do this? Paul explains,

"…if thy enemy hunger, feed him; if he thirst, give him drink: for in so doing thou shalt heap coals of fire on his head. Be not overcome of evil, but overcome evil with good." (Rom 12:20-21). Your acts of love are your swords against all evils targeted against you.

Thus, the only effective weapon of warfare against all forces of darkness attempting to keep you down is love. Use it and see how fast you will climb to the top. A man of God once said that the depth of your love determines the height you will reach in life. I completely agree with him.

Love is a sacrifice

To love, as God wants us to, is not an easy thing. It needs grace. That's why you need God. God is love. Our God is not a God of love, He *is* love. Love is the nature of God. God does not have love, possess love, acquire love or contain love. GOD is LOVE. Therefore, to be able to have this nature, one needs to obtain help from Him.

This help He has already made available to us, knowing beforehand that one day we would need it. This help is readily available through the assistance of the Holy Spirit. So Paul wrote,

"And hope maketh not ashamed; because the love of God is shed abroad in our hearts by the Holy Ghost which is given unto us." (Rom 5:5).

You want to get to the top. Fulfill the law. And since you cannot do it yourself, ask for the assistance of the all-time helper, the Holy Spirit. Remember, you cannot make it to the top without this vital nature of God, and God expects us to be clothed in this gown. As you cultivate this nature of God, I believe that your desires in God shall be speedily granted.

Love, which makes you to have the nature of God, prepares you for the next component of the fruit, joy.

CHAPTER TWELVE

JOY

"Joy is the spiritual sickle for harvesting
kingdom blessings"

While love is the nature of God, joy is the environment where God operates. Where joy is found, God always abides. But when joy is absent, God is conspicuously absent. Look at heaven where God's abode is, there is no weeping, sorrow, death, nor pain, but only happiness, joy and laughter. God plans to make the environment on earth identical to that of heaven before establishing His kingdom here on earth, so he plans to,

"wipe away all tears from their eyes; and there shall be no more death, neither sorrow, nor crying, neither shall there be any more pain: for the former things are passed away." (Rev 21:4). This is identical to the environment where God operates. This is why He asked us to always pray, "Let thy kingdom come." This is in preparation for His second coming.

On the other hand, sorrow is synonymous to satanic environment, where there is weeping and gnashing of teeth,

"The son of man shall send forth his angels, and they shall gather out of his kingdom all things that offend, and them which do iniquity; And shall cast them into a furnace of fire: there shall be wailing and gnashing of teeth." (Mt 13:41-42). Also see Luke 13:27-28. So, where there is weeping and gnashing of teeth, God is absent; and Satan is very much present.

To bring God into the affairs of your life, you need joy. And since God is the principal factor in kingdom excellence, the need for joy cannot be over emphasized.

Hear this.

One day, David and his men went to bring God – represented by the Ark of God – from a strange land back to the city of David. They forgot to prepare and to sanctify themselves. Above all, they left joy behind. God's anger kindled against Uzza, and He smote him, and he immediately died.

God did not smite him because he offered to prevent the Ark from falling. No. But because they left the compulsory requirement for God's favourable disposition - that is joy.

David got scared, decided to leave the Ark in Obed-edom's place for a while so that he may go and reconsider his ways. He discovered his grave mistake, which caused him the death of one of his trusted men.

Then he made amends. In 1 Chronicles 15, he prepared a place for the Ark of God, and pitched for it a tent. Also, he invited the right people – the Levites - to carry the Ark and requested them to sanctify themselves, so that the due order may be followed.

But more importantly,

"David spake to the chief of the Levites to appoint their brethren to be the singers with instruments of music, psalteries and harps and cymbals, sounding, by lifting up the voice with joy." (Vs 16). And so, they brought the Ark of the Covenant of the Lord out of the house of Obed-edom with joy. (Vs 25). This passage emphasizes the fact that joy tickles God.

How do you get joy?

Joy is not gotten from fasting, praying, sleeping in church, meditating or even reading the word but, Joy, like faith cometh. Once the spirit is fully developed and mature enough to bear fruits, then Joy will come,

"For his anger endureth but a moment; in his favour there is life: weeping may endure for a night, but joy cometh in the morning." (Ps 30:5). As long as His joy is absent, weeping continues; as long as the conditions are not ripe for joy to come, night continues. But once the person is fully developed in the spirit, joy comes, and weeping vanishes. The entrance of joy terminates God's anger, bringing His favour wherein there is life.

From where cometh joy?

Joy is made and found in heaven, and constitutes the environment of God. All true joy originates and comes from the Lord;

"Thou shall show me the path of life: in thy presence is fullness of joy; at thy right hand there are pleasures for evermore." (Ps 16:11). Because the fullness of joy is found in His presence, going up unto God's alter gives you an opportunity to be baptized with the spirit of joy.

"Then will I go unto the altar of God, unto God my exceeding joy:"(Ps 43:4). The spirit of joy freely comes to a spiritually mature Christian who is continually found in His presence. That was why David said,

"Blessed is the man that walketh not in the counsel of the ungodly, nor standeth in the way of sinners, nor sitteth in the seat of the scornful. But his delight is in the law of the Lord; and in his law doth he meditate day and night. And he shall be like a tree planted by the rivers of water, that bringeth forth his fruit in due season; his leaf shall not wither; and whatsoever he doeth shall prosper." (Ps 1:1-3). Staying with God brings the spirit of joy, which beautifies your destiny.

Joy has its benefits too.

Once the spirit of joy comes, life takes a new turn. The coming of joy delivers into your hands the key to the benefits of salvation.

"Therefore with joy shall ye draw water out of the wells of salvation." (Is: 12:3). All the benefits of salvation – good life, divine health, freedom from curses, prosperity, liberty, wisdom and all others – are only accessible through the key of joy. Without joy, you cannot draw anything from God. Many people are suffering today because they lack joy.

Yes, they have been born-again since time immemorial; they may have been-born again and again several times. But they are still under the yoke of sickness, poverty, curses, barrenness, etc., just because they have failed to draw what they need out of the well of God using the sickle of joy. As you allow yourself to be baptized by this spirit today, all that the enemy has stolen from you shall be returned in multiples, Amen.

Thus, to obtain the very best from God, make your house a house of joy, and your city a joyous city (Is 32:13).

When you have joy, you automatically enter into His fullness, because that's actually where joy stays. And when you are in His fullness, everything is possible to you. Joy grows. It behaves like a living thing. It may increase when nourished, or decrease and die if starved. Thus, when you walk into His fullness, do not relax; keep working on yourself, so that your joy like His own may be full. Hearken unto him, so that His joy may remain with you and your joy may be full.

"These things have I spoken unto you, that my joy might remain in you, and that your joy may be full." (Jn 15:11). Until it is full, it is not yet enough.

This is where many people usually miss it. This key comes to them, they think that they have apprehended, and before you know it, it is lost. That shall not be your portion in Jesus mighty name, Amen.

Evidence of joy.

How do you know that this great and wonderful spirit has come? The primary evidence of joy is gladness. Where the spirit of joy is there is gladness of heart.

"Thou has put gladness in my heart, more than in the time that their corn and their wine increased." (Ps 4:7). Joy brings the kind of gladness of heart that not even wealth and riches could give. This then strengthens you against your oppositions and detractors, for

"Then he said unto them, Go thy way, eat the fat, and drink the sweet, and send portions unto them for whom nothing is prepared: for this day is holy unto our Lord: neither be ye sorry; for the joy of the Lord is your strength." (Neh 8:10).Joy manifests in singing and praising God despite whatever the present circumstances may look like or what challenges you may be facing,

"Break forth into joy, sing together, ye waste places of Jerusalem: for the Lord hath comforted his people, he hath redeemed Jerusalem." (Is 52:9). Singing is a confirmation that you have truly found the joy of the Lord,

"Behold, my servants shall sing for joy of heart, but ye shall cry for sorrow of heart, and shall howl for vexation of spirit." (Is 65:14).

When the joy of the Lord is inside of your heart, you cannot hide it. It must show. And when you find it, you must share it with others, and like this woman, call others.

"And when she hath found it, she calleth her friends and her neighbors together, saying, Rejoice with me; for I have found the piece which I lost." (Lk: 15:9). Spread it, tell others about it, and tell them about the benefits of joy, then yours will multiply.

How to develop this key.

You may ask me, "How do I get this key?"

- Find the word of God, eat it, get baptized in the spirit of God, and as you nurture your faith and meditate on the word, the spirit of joy shall come. Hear this,

  "Thy words were found, and I did eat them; and thy words was unto me the joy and rejoicing of mine heart: for I am called by the name, O Lord God of hosts." (Jer 15:16).

  Above all, aim for the highest level of joy – joy unspeakable, full of glory-. That's actually what God desires for all of us. This is one of the benefits of salvation, just because you believed in Him,

  "Whom having not seen, ye love; in whom, though now ye see him not, yet believing, ye *(shall therefore)* rejoice with joy unspeakable and full of glory." (1 Pet 1:8).

- Be grateful. Count your blessings, name them one by one. And as you thank him, you shall find reason to remain grateful and joyful.
- Share your testimonies. Also meditate on the testimonies of others. Remember that the testimony of Jesus is the spirit of prophecy. (Rev 19:10). This also gives you a good reason to be joyful. It allows you to see that the Lord is faithful
- Watch who your friend is. For iron sharpeneth iron. (Prov 27:17). The kind of friends you make determines your level of joy. So make the right kind of friends. "He that walketh with wise men shall be wise: but a companion of fools shall be destroyed." (Prov: 13:20). Similarly, he that walketh with the joyful shall be joyful. Therefore, "Be not deceived: evil communications corrupt good manners." (1 Cor: 15:33). Watch out.

Joy reduces your struggles.

Let me shock you a little. Praying without ceasing is good, protracted fasting is wonderful, and all nights fasting and prayers are excellent; but if joy is absent, they are mere physical exercises. Why? Joy is the only thing that stimulates the Father, arrests His interest, and compels Him to hearken to our requests. It is only the joyful that the father hears.

Some great apostles, including Paul, used this principle. For instance, Paul revealing the secrets of his exploits in prayer said,

"I thank my God upon every remembrance of you, Always in every prayer of mine for you all making request with joy." (Phil: 1:3-4). Thus, apart from praying for others, which is a vital key for captivity turning, more importantly, you must make all your requests with joy. It worked for Paul; it shall also work for you.

Those that used this key.

Let me now show you some kingdom stars that excelled through the key of joy. The very first is Joseph. You must have heard about his great dreams and visions, and how he went from nakedness to pit, from pit to Potiphar's place, from Potiphar's place to prison, and from prison to the palace.

Have you ever asked yourself about what kept him going all these while? Let me tell you, it is JOY. Joy made him to be described as a goodly person and this brought a lot of favour his way (Gen 39:6). No wonder he was able to notice the sad countenance of his fellow prisoner one early morning. It is only a joyful man that can notice the absence of joy in others. Here this,

"And Joseph came in unto them in the morning, and looked upon them, and, behold, they were sad." (Gen 40:6). It was this single encounter that later turned his whole captivity around, when one of the men remembered him in the palace. Because joy ventilates the brain, he was able to hear God and to interpret the men's dreams, an act that made him famous. And as you go for this key, every captivity in your life shall turn to liberty.

David was also another man that made great use of this key. Remember where we read from in 1 Chronicles chapters 13 and 15. He needed joy to bring back the Ark of the Covenant to the city of David. Also, you remember when the ark was on its way to Jerusalem, David's joy knew no bounds. He danced and rejoiced that even his own wife, Michal despised him (2 Sam 6:16). This he did, and very well too that all of his Psalms were either psalms of praise, worship and/or thanksgiving. No wonder God Himself had to testify about him, saying;

"I have found David my servant;" (Ps 89:20); and promised to establish him, fight for him, plague all his enemies, and decorate him with His faithfulness and mercy. He started fulfilling this promise by making Michal barren for life. As you dwell in God's presence through joy, God will also find you, boast about you, and fight your battles for you.

Then let us look at our saviour, Jesus. He was also a saviour full of joy. He always created an environment of joy. He gave His disciples nicknames like Peter (the rock) for Simeon. As if this was not enough, he always rejoiced at the great doings of God. Remember the time he sent out His disciples two by two for fieldwork in evangelism, the Bible recorded,

"And the seventy returned again with joy, saying, Lord, even the devils are subject unto us through your name. In that hour Jesus rejoiced in spirit," (Lk 10:17,21). Jesus needed the ever-abiding presence of God the father to fulfill His mission on earth, and He knew how to keep Him always by His side – through joy. Today joy will bring God present to that your situation. And as He comes, joy will keep Him always around you.

Did you notice that the above scripture said that the apostles returned with joy? The joy of the Master Jesus was infectious. Nobody could stay near Him without being joyful, so He had a way of making all around Him joyful.

Paul is another kingdom star that knew the value of joy. In all his letters, he kept on emphasizing on the need for joy and rejoicing. Hear him,

"Rejoice in the Lord always: and again I say, Rejoice." (Phil 4:4)

"Finally, my brethren, rejoice in the Lord." (Phil 3:1).

"Rejoice evermore." (1 Thess 5:16). His advice on joy is everywhere. If Paul was a kingdom star, joy took him there. The secrets of a man are found in his speeches. He knows the value of joy.

Just like Joseph, David, Jesus and Paul, as you tap into this kingdom key, your shinning shall appear to all.

Do you really trust God?

If you do, and you believe that your expectations in Him shall not be cut off; neither will His words that have gone out of His mouth concerning you return unfulfilled, then prophesy this passage from Isaiah over yourself,

"I will greatly rejoice in the Lord, my soul shall be joyful in my God; for He hath clothed me with the garment of salvation,

He hath covered me with the robe of righteousness, as a bridegroom decked himself with ornaments, and as a bride adorneth herself with her jewels…and as the garden causeth the things that are sown in it to spring forth; so the Lord will cause *(my)* righteousness and praise to spring forth before all the nations." (Is 61:10-11). As you have said in His ears, so will He do for you (Num 14:28).

Do you know that Biblical prophecies are the most potent forms of prophecies? It is just reminding the King of kings what he said concerning you. God shall surely fulfill His words in your life in the mighty name of Jesus Christ, Amen.

CHAPTER THIRTEEN

PEACE

"Without the peace of God
Kingdom excellence is an illusion."

God is not just a God of love and joy, but also of peace. This is at least what the Bible has made us to understand from several parts of the scripture. For instance, Paul wrote,

"Finally brethren, farewell. Be perfect, be of good comfort, be of one mind, live in peace; and the God of love and peace shall be with you." (2 Cor 13:11). So having the key of love without the key of peace is having only one part of the key, like having the key without the padlock.

Peace defined.

Peace talks about calm response to issues of life, a life that is free of strife, discord, conflicts, trouble, contention, dissension, and rivalry; or a life in which there is full harmony in personal relationships, especially with God. Peace is living a concern free life, a war free existence, a life of joy and love.

114

Peace like joy comes to those that have a full and unshakable trust in God. Without total trust in the ability of God to take adequate care of one's problems, peace cannot be found. For,

"I will both lay me down in peace, and sleep: for thou, Lord, only makest me dwell in safety." (Ps 4:8). It is only those that completely trust God that can say just what the Psalmist has just said.

Peace is a fruit.

Peace is therefore a product of your belief. If you believe in the Son of God, His peace through the Holy Spirit shall be given unto you as He promised.

"Peace I leave with you, my peace I give unto you: not as the world giveth, give I unto you. Let not your hearts be troubled, neither let it be afraid." (Jn 14:27). He is saying, 'I will only give you my peace if your hearts are stayed on me and nothing else, if you totally trust in me, believe in me, and are not moved by the circumstances around you.' Do you need this key? Then trust Him with all your heart.

It is actually to deliver this key to Christians that made Christ to come. The birth of Jesus Christ terminated every war and crisis of life. It connotes the birth of peace and goodwill to all men. Please see Isaiah 9:6-7and Luke 2:8-20.

But, like love and joy, peace is a fruit and not a gift. It is worked for. Therefore, seek peace from the Lord, for it is only from Him that real peace could be gotten. No wonder, Moses said,

"The Lord lift up His countenance upon thee, and <u>give thee peace</u>." (Num 6:26). When the Lord sees your faith and trust in Him, he favours you with the spirit of peace.

"Depart from evil, and do good; seek peace, and pursue it." (Ps 34:14). Peace needs to be sought after, needs to be pursued. But only those that are righteous, those that have departed from evil, those that have a right standing with God are the ones qualified to seek and pursue it.

Are you therefore qualified? If you are not, it is still not too late, you can make amends now, and God will gladly forgive and forget all your past sins. Do it now, and experience the peace of God that passeth all understanding. Apostle Peter in his attempt to confirm the importance of righteousness, wrote,

"Let him *(that needs God kind of peace)* eschew *(turn away from)* evil, and do good; let him seek peace *(for it is not a gift),* and ensue *(pursue)* it." (1 Pet 3:11).

Peace access routes.

You may be asking yourself now, "How can I obtain this fruit of the Holy spirit?" let me show you five ways by which you can access this vital fruit;

1. **Salvation** is the visa to the peace of God. Anyway, I know that you know by now that the peace of God is a fruit of the Holy Spirit. Let me then tell you that

the Holy Spirit can only dwell in a holy temple – a body that has been washed and redeemed by the precious blood of Jesus Christ. This fruit is therefore reserved for the true sons of God; no wonder the Psalmist said,

"The Lord will give strength unto his people; the Lord will bless his people with peace." (Ps 29:11). The Lord will bless, not everybody, but only His people – the saved ones – with peace. To emphasize this, he again said,

"I will hear what God the Lord will speak: for he will speak peace unto his people, and to his saints:" (Ps 85:8). God only speaks and blesses His people. The door is still open, and His arms are still wide open. Paul also wrote,

"Therefore being justified by faith, we have peace with God through our Lord Jesus Christ:" (Rom 5:1). So it is only after you have been justified through faith in Jesus Christ that you have this peace. I pray that you will judge yourself, and if you really need salvation, please run to the Master for help. And as you do this, even now, I prophesy a change in your situation and circumstances.

2. **Seek God**. Being saved is very important, but it is not all that is needed to obtain peace from God. Salvation is the gate pass, while seeking God delivers it into your hands.

Pant after God and the things of God, thirst to know him more every day of your life. If you were saved just to go to heaven, God would have allowed you to sleep and join Him the same day you got born again. That He left you here means that he has a purpose for your life, and that is fellowship. Therefore, like David, pant and thirst after God. David understood the benefits of this step, thus he wrote,

"As the deer panteth after the water brooks, so panteth my soul after thee, O God. My soul thirsteth for God, for the living God: when will I come and appear before God?" (Ps 42:1-2). To buttress his fact, he also said,

"O God, thou art my God; early will I seek thee: my soul thirsteth for thee, my flesh longeth for thee in a dry and thirsty land, where no water is…My soul followeth hard after thee: thy right hand upholdeth me." (Ps 63:1,8). Hear him again,

"My soul longeth, yea, even fainteth for the courts of the Lord: my heart and my flesh crieth out for the living God." (Ps 84:2).

You have no choice if you really need peace but to seek, search, long after and cry for God, "For he is our peace, who hath made both one, and hath broken down the middle wall of partition between us;" (Eph 2:14).

There was a man who sought God with all his heart. His name was Asa in 2 Chronicles 14. After the death of his father, Abijah, he reigned in his father's stead. He did what was right in the eyes of the Lord his God, he took away the altars of strange gods, and the high places, and broke down the images, and cut down the groves: and commanded Judah to seek the Lord of their fathers, and to do the commandment. He also took away out of all Judah the high places and the images. Due to these his God seeking moves, the kingdom was quite before him and he was able to build fenced cities in Judah, and it was recorded concerning his reign and time saying,

"for the land had rest, and he had no war in those years; because the Lord *(who he sought after)* had given him rest." Seeing what God has done, he confessed, "because we have sought the Lord our God, we have sought Him, and He hath given us rest on every side." (2 Chron 14:6-7). The peace they found made them to build and prosper.

As you too seek God, you shall find Him; and when you do, you shall have rest round about, you shall build and you shall likewise prosper in Jesus name.

3. **Pray for Peace**: Like wisdom, peace can be prayed for. The Bible enjoins us all to,

"Pray for the peace of Jerusalem: *(then)* **they shall prosper that love thee.** *(Pray that)* **peace** *(shall be)* **within thy walls, and prosperity within thy palaces. For my brethren and companions'** *(who have prayed)* **sake, I** *(the Lord who you prayed*

to) will now say, Peace be within thee." (Ps 122:6-8). Prayer can therefore make God to release his own type of peace. This is because God blesses His people with peace. Remember what the Psalmist said, "The Lord will give strength unto His people; The Lord will bless His people with peace." (Ps 29:11). And He only blesses those that ask. Ask!

4. **Declare Peace always**: You can declare it and it shall come into existence. The Bible said,

"When thou comest nigh unto a city to fight against it, then proclaim peace unto it." (Deut 20:10). The spirit of God helps us to do this more effectively. That is, it is those that are already baptized in the Holy Ghost that can properly declare peace. There is a good example in the Bible. His name is Amasai. When Amasai and his men wanted to join the camp of David, he had to declare to be accepted.

"Then the spirit came upon Amasai, who was chief of the captains, and he said...peace, peace be unto thee, and peace be to thine helpers;" (1 Chron 12:18). And as you chose to declare today and always, no devil shall be able to tamper with your peace anymore.

Let me bring something to your notice. Peace has a companion called prosperity. Look at Asa from the passage we read before. When he had peace round about, he and his men built, and the Bible said, "so they build and prospered." (2 Chron 14:7).

Look at this wonderful greeting from David to Nabal in 1 Samuel 25 vs. 6,

"And thus shall ye say to him that liveth in prosperity, Peace be both to thee, and peace be to thine house, and peace be unto all that thou hast." What he was actually saying was, "because you have peace in yourself, your house and all around you, you now live in prosperity". As you declare your peace in God, your own prosperity shall be made manifest to all men.

5. **Preach the Gospel of God**: Preaching the word makes God continually present with you. When you make it a habit to witness to people always about Christ, His presence abides with you. And when He comes, He does not come alone, but with the Holy Spirit, to confirm your words with signs following; like He did with the early apostles. See this in Mark 16:20,

   "And they went forth, and preached everywhere, the Lord working with them, and confirming the word with signs following." This is actually a confirmation of His promise in Matthew 28:19-20, where He said,

   "Go ye therefore, and teach all nations, baptizing them in the name of the Father, and of the Son, and of the Holy Ghost: Teaching them to observe all things whatsoever I have commanded you: and, lo, I am with you always, even unto the end of the world." That means that divine presence is an exclusive preserve of those that obey this commandments, to preach the word. They do not need to pray, fast or worry themselves about it. As long as they preach the word, the presence of God is guaranteed. Paul, emphasizing what Isaiah prophesied, said,

"How beautiful are the feet of them that preach the gospel of peace, and bring glad tidings of good things." (Rom 10:15). As long as you preach the glad tidings, peace is part of your reward. Remember, the master Himself said,

"the labourer is worthy of his hire." (Lk 10:7). He who made the law cannot owe you your wages. I see Him paying you all your wages with extra as you go for His peace today.

Three things you must do.

When this important fruit has started developing, there are three things you must do.

1. **Allow it to multiply**. Peace can actually multiply. To this Peter advised,

   "Grace and peace be multiplied unto you through the knowledge of God, and of Jesus our Lord." (2 Pet 1:2). He said that the instrument of this multiplication is the knowledge of God and of His Son, Jesus. So, go for knowledge; and as you go, I see your peace being severally multiplied.

2. **Hold and guard your peace**. Do not allow it to be stolen. It could be stolen, if you take it for granted. That you have peace today does not mean that you will have peace forever. So guard it jealously with all your might. Otherwise the birds of the air, the enemies of destiny, and the ants of life may either destroy it or steal it away. Like the Psalmist, hold your peace. (Ps 39:2).

How do you hold your peace? This is very simple. Let your mind be stayed on God. As long as you are connected to your source, you remain resourceful. As long as your mind is stayed on God, your peace stays with you. Here this,

"Thou will keep him in perfect peace, whose mind is stayed on thee: because he trusteth in thee." (Is 26:3). Therefore, if perfect peace is what you desire, trust God completely, and let your trust cause your mind to stay on Him. And as you do this, peace perfect peace shall never depart from your habitation.

3. Now that you have found this peace, have allowed it to multiply, and have protected it from adversaries of life and destiny, allow it to rule and keep your hearts and minds. That is the only way you can achieve kingdom excellence. This is because it is only a peaceful heart and mind that can invent, build and develop things that will attract people's attention. Where there is no peace, there can never be any prosperity. Go for peace; but more importantly, allow

the peace you have found to work in you and help you grow. Now, as you decide to do this, I see **the peace of God, which passeth all understanding, keep your hearts and minds through Christ Jesus. Amen. (Phil 4:7).**

Peace procures kingdom excellence.

How does this very important key procure kingdom excellence? These are what I chose to call the benefits of this vital fruit. Let me give you a few.

✓ Peace commits God to your affairs. It secures supernatural attention.

"Be still, and know that I am God: I will be exalted among the heathen, I will be exalted in the earth." (Ps 46:10). God only exalts Himself in a life where peace – stillness – exists.

✓ Peace provokes supernatural intervention. Without peace, God will never manifest His powers. Hear His instruction to those that needed His assistance in a time of war;

"Ye shall not need to fight in this battle: set yourselves, stand ye still, and see the salvation of the Lord with you," (2 Chron 20:17). Until you stand still, you will not see God in action. Do you know why He loves it this way? It is so that all glory may come unto Him. He does not want to share (nor give) His glory with (to) anyone else. This is why He said,

"I am the Lord: that is my name: and my glory will I not give to another, neither my praise to graven images. (Is 42:8). So just stand still, be at peace, and then God will work for you.

✓ From the passage we read in Psalm 122 from verse 7, we saw that peace also enhances mental excellence, creativity, innovations, and productivity. These will then lead to prosperity within thy palaces. Especially when peace is within your walls – the walls of your heart and mind.

What then is God saying?

God is saying, "Behold, I will extend peace to her (YOU) like a river...As one whom his mother comforteth, so will I comfort you...And when ye shall see this, your hearts shall rejoice, and your bones shall flourish like an herb;" (Is 66:12-14). But you have a choice, to accept or refuse this His precious offer. I pray that you shall accept His offer by obeying all you have read on how to cultivate this fruit. And as you do, the Lord God "will make a covenant of peace with them (YOU);" and this covenant of peace "shall be an everlasting covenant..." and He will place and bless you, and multiply you and dwell in your midst forever. (Ezek 37:26).

CHAPTER FOURTEEN

PATIENCE

"Patience protects the seed and patience
preserves the harvest."

In our anchor scripture, the word patience is represented by longsuffering. This is to emphasize the fact that sometimes, patience can actually involve a long period of waiting, which some people may take as a period of suffering. But the fact is that, in truth, every promise of God has a maturation date. The period between the promise and the maturation and subsequent manifestation vary from one promise to the other. It is actually within this period that patience is expected and required.

Patience is vital.

Patience is not a gift, it is a virtue. There are NO miracles from God without patience, even for supposedly instant miracles. People who lack patience miss their miracles. Let me re-iterate that patience is not a gift; it is a fruit that must be developed for full manifestation of the promises of God.

Take a seed for instance. Every word that God drops in our life is like a seed. So, also is every kingdom discovery. Even prophecies are seeds. And like the natural seed, if it abides alone, it will not prosper; but if it is planted in the soil (similar to accepting the word of God and believing that it will work for you), over time, it germinates, grows, matures and bears fruits. Same is the word that we hear.

As you do not just plant your seeds and go home to come back on the harvest day, but will come regularly to weed, water, and tend the garden for a bumper harvest, and sometimes eliminate insects and other farm pests that want to destroy your plantings; so are you expected to handle things of the spirit. You must water your garden (using confessions of your mouth), you must weed your garden (standing against all adversaries that may be blocking your open door, or any Satan that may be trying to withstand you from obtaining your harvest), you must guard against any discouragements, faithlessness and unbelief that may rub you of your profiting and you must fight any stronghold of the devil or imaginations that may negatively impact on your harvest.

The kind of investment you put into the growth and development of the seed determines the type of harvest you take home at the end of the farming season.

Waiting, after having done all, is not wasting!

Just like you do not harvest the same day you planted, also, in the things of the spirit, you may not obtain the result immediately. As you will be willing to wait for a season before coming back to harvest from your farmland, you should also be willing to wait, (most times the need may arise for you to wait in prayers), for a time before collecting your answers.

The waiting time is not a waste; it is for maturity of your harvest. It is during this period that you need patience. It is only those that have developed the fruit of patience that usually go home with their harvest fully matured. Some impatient people collect their fruits before full maturation, while others may even abort the harvest by their actions or even inactions.

Patience explained.

Patience talks about endurance, forbearance, longsuffering, allowing God to bring out the blessings at His own appointed time; that is, when all things have been made beautiful, for

"He hath made everything beautiful in His time; also He hath set the world in their heart, so that no man can find out the work that God maketh from the beginning to the end." (Eccl 3:11).

You have not the ability to know what He has decided to do and when, but trust Him enough to believe that He will give you the very best; that is faith. It is this understanding that yields patience, knowing that,

"Whatever God doeth, it shall be forever: nothing can be put to it, nor anything taken from it," (Eccl 3:14). This is the foundation of patience.

God performs His wonders at His own time, not your time; in His own way, not your way; and by His own pattern, not yours. A good understanding of this makes it a lot easier to allow God enough room to do His things.

Patience therefore requires us to continually rest on the Lord, waiting upon Him for the best of life like the Psalmist said,

"Rest in the Lord, and wait patiently for Him: fret not thyself because of him who prospereth in his way, because of the man who bringeth wicked devices to pass." (Ps 37:7). Rest on the Lord. Develop your faith in Him and then patience will be so easily manifested that people will envy you and your testimonies in God.

Why patience?

It is only people that have patience that bring in good fruits. Looking again at the natural seeds, different seeds have different maturing time. Some bear fruits within the same year and are harvested (e.g. maize). But they also wither within the same year. Others take a longer time to bear fruits (e.g. orange) and they last several years bearing fruits. Thus, the period between planting and fruit bearing plays a significant role in the kind of fruits and how long the fruits are produced. No wonder the Bible said concerning the word,

"But that on the good ground are they, which in an honest heart, having heard the word, keep it, and bring forth fruit with patience." (Lk 8:15). To bring forth fruits via the word, there is first of all the acceptance of the word, followed by the keeping of the same till the appointed time, and then using the kept word to produce results when the due time comes.

Every promise of God usually has a waiting period. This period, like for seeds, vary greatly depending on the kind of dividends expected. Take for instance, the passage that said, "Whoso findeth a wife findeth a good thing, and obtaineth favour of the Lord" (Prov 18:22). The passage said 'whoso' and this includes anybody – a child, a teenager, adolescence, and an adult. However, will a child because the word has promised divine favour for whoso findeth, start looking for a wife at ten years of age to obtain this favour? That will be seen to be wrong.

Similarly, it will be wrong for the same child to be praying using Genesis 2:18, where God talked about it not being good for a man to be alone. An orphan or an only child can use this passage to pray for companionship, but absolutely not for a life partner at that age. However, if he does pray for a life partner, God will still hear him, but the waiting period will be longer. It is actually advisable for children to be taught to start early to pray for their life partners, so as to give God sufficient time to completely overhaul their life partners. But believing that God will bring the person to them to marry each other immediately may be out of the question.

So, although God has promised everyone a life partner, like other blessings of His, there is always a waiting period. No wonder Jesus told the disciples,

"Wait for the promise of the Father, which, saith He, ye have heard of me." (Acts 1:4).

Lack of patience has actually wrecked some lives. You need patience to run the race of life.

"Wherefore seeing that we also are compassed about with so great a cloud of witnesses, let us lay aside every weight, and the sin which doth so easily beset us, and let us run with patience the race that is set before us. Looking unto Jesus the author and finisher of our faith" (Heb 12:1-2). So, even Jesus the master Himself had patience. You need it too.

Patience delivers God's promises to us – fully beautified and with necessary icing. Talking about Abraham, the Bible had this testimony of him,

"And so, after he had patiently endured, he obtained the promise." (Heb 6:15). You too can obtain with patience, and I see you obtaining in Jesus name.

Furthermore, patience has a way of wiping away every shame and reproach in people's lives. Looking at Abraham again, his patience changed his fatherlessness, which was very shameful, to a "father of many nations". That was why the Bible boldly said,

"And not only so, but we glory in tribulations also: knowing that tribulations worketh patience; And patience, experience; and experience, hope: And hope maketh not ashamed;" (Rom 5:3-5). Patience at times of tribulations gives God enough room to wipe away all shame and reproach. As you give God an opportunity to work unhindered, every reproach in your life shall be wiped away.

Run from impatience.

Therefore, "thou, O man of God, flee these things; and follow after righteousness, godliness, faith, patience, meekness. Fight the good fight of faith, lay hold on eternal life," (1 Tim 6:11). Flee impatience, embrace patience; this is the mark of a mature Christian. Are you a mature Christian? Then, obey the scriptures, which said;

"That the aged men be sober, grave, temperate, sound in faith, in charity, in patience." (Tit 2:2).

You may be asking me by now, "How do I cultivate patience?" The answer is very simple. Have total and unalloyed faith in God, believe that He is able to fulfill that which He has promised, that he will never mismanage your life, that he makes everything beautiful at His own time, and see patience grow seamlessly.

Some have walked this path.

Let me show you some great men that made it through patience. We have talked extensively about Abraham. But look at Noah. Noah after hearing from God, had to build an ark for 120 years – not days, not weeks, and not months – but years; that is over forty-three thousand, eight hundred and thirty (43,830) days; that is over one million, fifty-one thousand, two hundred (1,051,200) hours.

He must have been the subject of ridicule in his time, but he continued until the day the rain started. Even when he started collecting animals for preservation, who knows what people must have said concerning him. However, at last, who smiled, Noah. So, it does not matter what people are saying, as long as you are on course with God, you shall have the final laugh. The delay may be deliberate, but the destination is sure.

Jacob worked for fourteen years before he could marry the woman of his dreams – Rachel. (Gen 29:20-28). He waited patiently for this length of years to marry her. Is it surprising, therefore, that it was a child of this woman, Rachel that delivered them all from famine? Just imagine what would have happened if he did not wait!

The time you spend truly waiting on God is a great investment into your future. I see you reaping the full benefits in a short while. Meanwhile, while he was waiting, God did something. God gave him Leah. To him then it made no sense. But this woman ended up being the mother of six tribes of Israel, and her maid also became the mother of another two tribes. One of these tribes is Judea. You do know that Jesus Christ is of the tribe of Judea.

David was anointed a king very early in life. But he waited patiently for fifteen years to become thirty years before mounting the throne (2 Sam 5:4-5). Even when he had a chance to kill the usurper, Saul, he saved his life. Knowing that he was the rightful occupant of the throne, backed by God, he could have staged a coup de tat. But he didn't.

He even at a time became a servant in the house of Saul. This enabled him to learn how kings behaved, acted and handled situations. This earned him God's love and protection. He could therefore say,

"I waited for the Lord; and He inclined unto me, and heard my cry. He brought me up also out of an horrible pit, out of the miry clay, and set my feet upon a rock, and established my goings. And he has put a new song in my mouth." (Ps 40:1-3). No wonder he advised every Christian to,

"Wait on the Lord: be of good courage, and He shall strengthen thine heart: wait, I say, on the Lord." (Ps 27:14). This advice was because he knew that,

"The eyes of the Lord are upon the righteous, and His ears are open unto their cry. The righteous cry, and the Lord heareth, and delivereth them out of all their troubles." (Ps 34:15,17).

Mordecai is another good example of a man with patience who waited on the Lord. After waiting for several years, his situation changed. God remembered him. And because God remembered him, the king of the land could not sleep. And overnight his status changed. You have waited too. I do not know for how long. But one thing I am so sure of is this; that God shall surely remember you as He did remember Mordecai. As He turns to you, everything shall turn for you.

It is your turn, embrace this vital fruit and God will take you Himself to the topmost Amen.

CHAPTER FIFTEEN

GENTLENESS

"Let the gentle breeze blow
Let all trees bear their fruits."

Gentleness talks about being mild, calm and kind in actions and activities. Beyond this it talks of calmness of the mind, spirit and body. This is the full extent of gentleness.

Gentleness is a very important characteristic of the Holy Spirit. It is not uncommon to hear people refer to Him as the gentle Spirit. This is because in all its manifestations, gentleness is seen. You remember when He descended upon Jesus after Christ baptism as a dove. The dove is a very gentle bird, no wonder the Holy Spirit took the form of a dove to appear in the river of Jordan (Mt 3:16).

Sometimes the Spirit has been likened to the anointing, which represent another gentle and refreshing move of God. Even when the apostles were baptized, the Spirit descended as a tongue of fire, turning them into new men and refreshing their lives.

Thus, God in the form of the Holy Spirit has this fruit and desires all His children who are baptized in the Holy Spirit to manifest it. However, although it comes along with the Spirit at Holy Ghost baptism, you need to activate it, nurture and cultivate it for its fullness to be made manifest.

You need it!

You may be wondering why you must manifest this fruit to achieve kingdom excellence. The answer is very simple. Of all the fruits of the Spirit, gentleness is the only one linked directly with "becoming great". Gentleness is the mother of greatness.

So, if greatness is your desire, gentleness is your visa and pathway. David, recognizing that he became great in life by the instrumentality of gentleness said,

"Thou hast given me the shield of thy salvation: and thy right hand hath holden me up, and thy gentleness hath made me great." (Ps 18:35). Also see 2 Samuel 22:36.

It is not, therefore, salvation that made David great, after all he even knew very little about salvation, but God's gentleness. If salvation did not make him great, that means that it will not also make you great.

Salvation brings you into partnership with God; gentleness delivers God's blessings and favour upon you, thus providing what you need to become great.

Truly, you have no choice.

Do you know why you must be gentle? The Bible said,

"Can two walk together, except they be agreed?" (Amos 3:3). You cannot walk with God nor enjoy His blessings in full if you are not like Him. God is often pictured as a shepherd, gently caring for and guiding His flock. God is very powerful and mighty, yet gentle and careful. Hear this,

"Behold, the Lord God will come with strong hand, and His arm shall rule for Him...He shall feed His flock like a shepherd: He shall gather the lambs with his arm, and carry them in His bosom, and shall gently lead those that are with young." (Is 40:10-11). So, a gentle lifestyle is a cardinal prerequisite to enter into the fullness of God. Paul understood this fact, and used this key so well that he can even boast about it, and thus he wrote,

"But we were gentle among you, even as a nurse cherisheth her children." (1 Thess 2:7). This explains why God had to distinguish him from the rest, despite his shortcomings. Today as you cultivate this wonderful fruit, God shall likewise distinguish you among your peers.

Do you desire to be used greatly of God, as He used Paul? Then cultivate this fruit. Paul knew the benefits of gentleness, especially in the ministry. So, while advising prospective ministers of God, and any one desiring to be a servant of God, he said

"And the servant of the Lord must not strive; but be gentle unto all men, apt to teach, patient," (2 Tim 2:24). This is very vital for kingdom exploits and excellence.

Therefore, in all thy ways, be "...gentle," (Tit 3:2). This is all it takes for kingdom greatness.

Once the Spirit comes, one of the things He carries along is wisdom, which has gentleness as one of its characteristics. To manifest this trait requires full manifestation of the wisdom of God. We have the mind of Christ, so we also have the wisdom of Christ. Therefore, stir it up today and watch it take you to your high places on the earth.

CHAPTER SIXTEEN

GOODNESS

"Goodness procures godly favours"

This is the very next fruit of the spirit. Without this, the fruit is so incomplete and therefore unable to perform its functions.

What is goodness?

Goodness talks about someone showing kindness, being profitable to someone else, possessing excellent character and attitude, having a way of life that is fitting or appropriate to the societal norms, expectations and traditions, and living a morally upright life.

To be good is not a gift from God neither is it natural; it is therefore not anybody's nature, but a fruit to be cultivated. Without it, one cannot really claim to be godly. This I believe is based on the fact that God has 'abundant goodness' as one of His cardinal characteristics. Hear Him. While speaking of Himself, He said,

"I will make all my goodness pass before thee, and I will proclaim the name of the Lord before thee; and will be gracious to whom I will be gracious, and will show my mercy on whom I will show mercy."(Ex 33:19). In fulfillment of this promise, "the Lord passed by before him, and proclaimed, "The Lord, The Lord God, merciful and gracious, longsuffering, and abundant in goodness and truth," (Ex 34:6).

Actually, God's goodness is not available to all. It is an exclusive preserve of those that fear and put all their trust in Him. It is primarily for those who are willing to confess Him before others. The Psalmist, wrote,

"Oh how great is thy goodness, which thou hast laid up for them that fear thee; which thou hast wrought for them that trust in thee before the sons of men!"(Ps 31:19).

To such people, God usually decorates their lives with His great goodness. Talking about the children of Israel for instance, who were willing in certain situations to fight for the course of their God, the Bible recorded that

"so they did eat, and were filled, and became fat, and delighted themselves in thy great goodness." (Neh 9:25).

This fruit is not a one-time affair. It is a continuous requirement for the full manifestation of its benefits. Just like God, your goodness is expected to endure forever.

"Why boastest thou thyself in mischief, O mighty man? The goodness of God endureth continually." (Ps 52:1).

Goodness is it.

You may now be asking yourself, 'how important is this c fruit for my kingdom excellence?' The Bible in Ephesians summarized the fruits of the Spirit into three. Goodness is one of them. Not just one of them, actually the very first mentioned.

"For the fruit of the Spirit is in all goodness and righteousness and truth." (Eph 5:9).

Apart from being a necessary requirement for the full manifestation of the fruit of the Spirit, goodness makes rich. Despising the riches of His goodness can actually lead to poverty. (Rom 2:4). It also enhances productivity – especially of good fruits;

"A good tree cannot bring forth evil fruit, neither can a corrupt tree bring forth good fruit."(Mt 7:18).

Moreover, only pure minds think and behave like God; for "Unto the pure all things are pure: but unto them that are defiled and unbelieving is nothing pure; but even their mind and conscience is defiled."(Tit 1:15).Goodness brings you nearer God via pure thoughts and godly actions.

In addition, you cannot achieve what Christ achieved without this component fully operational in your life. For Christ was goodness exemplified. Hear Him,

"I am the good shepherd: and good shepherd giveth his life for the sheep." (Jn 10:11). And this He did on Calvary cross.

Road to goodness.

Now let me answer another question that is presently disturbing you; that is, 'how do I cultivate this fruit?' Once you are born again, you have access to the garden of goodness. However, you have a vital function to perform to cultivate this fruit. And that is to yield yourself completely to the shepherding of Jesus. Once you allow God to be your shepherd, goodness follows. Remember Psalm 23? When the Lord becomes your shepherd, then you shall not want any good thing. In addition to all the benefits of His shepherd-ship, surely

"goodness and mercy shall follow me all the days of my life:"(Ps 23:6). Not just for a day, few days, weeks, months or even years, but all the days of your life – as long as He remains your shepherd. This is the easiest means of cultivating this fruit. Allow Him today and see what He will do with your life. I see a total transformation in your life now and forever.

How to measure your goodness level.

When this component is fully developed, your attitude to people changes, for

"A good man showeth favour, and lendeth: he will guide his affairs with discretion." (Ps 112:5).

Job and Joseph are major Biblical examples of people who were extremely good. Hear their records,

For Job, the Bible recorded "There was a man in the land of Uz, whose name was Job; and that man was perfect and upright, and one that feared God, and eschewed evil." (Job 1:1). And for Joseph, It recorded, "And Joseph was a goodly person, and well favoured." (Gen 39:6).

You know very well how these two persons ended their journey on earth – very great and fulfilled. That is excellently well. If you desire what they had, then you must do what they did. Be goodly and let goodness become your middle name.

Once this component is fully at work, your rise to the top is guaranteed.

I pray that you shall embrace this key and move steadily to the top.

CHAPTER SEVENTEEN

FAITH

"That you are not seeing it,
does not mean that it is not there."

This is a very important fruit of the spirit. It is actually the bedrock on which the potentials of the entire fruit lies. Faith has several definitions and different meanings to different people. The Bible defines faith as,

"The substance of things hoped for, the evidence of things not seen." (Heb 11:1). Bishop David Oyedepo defined faith as "a living force, from a living word that produces living proofs."

In this discussion, I have looked at faith as an acronym meaning "Failing to Accept Insinuations that Trample on Heaven's plans and programs for a man." That is refusing to accept any initiative, imagination or suggestion that is counter covenant, ungodly or that may mitigate your chances of getting to heaven or enjoying heaven's provisions on earth.

144

Faith pleases God.

Faith commits God and turns His attention towards your affairs. This fruit specializes in pleasing God, for,

"But without faith it is impossible to please Him: for he that cometh to God must first believe that He is, and that He is a rewarder of them that diligently seek Him." (Heb 11:6). Since without faith it is impossible to please God, it therefore means that with faith, one can please Him. Faith does not only commit God, or stops at converting the written words into the power of God for effective miracles, it also protects us from sin as...

"And he that doubteth is damned...for whatsoever is not of faith is sin." (Rom 14:23). So walking in faith is walking in righteousness, no wonder it pleases God.

Benefits of faith.

Faith pleases God and therefore procures profiting in the kingdom. Without faith, profiting is impossible;

"For unto us was the gospel preached, as well as unto them: but the word preached did not profit them, not being mixed with faith in them that heard it." (Heb 4:2).

For instance, it is through the avenue of faith that we inherit God's promises. Thus, we are enjoined,

"ye be not slothful, but followers of them who through faith and patience inherit promises." (Heb 6:12). These promises, which I call the benefits of faith, include:

- By faith we live. Without faith, therefore, spiritual (and even physical death) is inevitable. For "the just shall live by his faith." (Hab 2:4). Also see Romans 1:17; Galatians 3:11; and Hebrews 10:38.
- By faith we are justified. Justification is not a product of good works, but of faith. "Knowing that a man is not justified by the works of the law, but by the faith of Jesus Christ, even we have believed in Jesus Christ, that we might be justified by faith of Christ, not by works of the law: for by the works of the law shall no man be justified." (Gal 2:16). Thus, it is only deep-rooted belief in Christ borne out of faith in Him that justifies. Also see Romans 3:28 for the conclusion of the matter. No wonder, therefore, the Master speaking to a woman who everybody knew was a sinner, but seeing the faith in her, said; "Thy faith hath saved thee; go in peace." (Lk 7:50). Faith saves!
- By faith we are sanctified. In Acts of the Apostles, it is written; "To open their eyes, and to turn from darkness, and from the power of Satan unto God, that they may receive forgiveness of sins, and inheritance among them which are sanctified by faith that is in me." (Acts 26:18).
- By faith we stand. "For by faith ye stand." (2 Cor 1:24). Standing right with God and man is therefore a product of your faith in God.
- By faith we are kept – kept from all challenges and evils of the world, preserved from the decadence, excused from the corruption prevalent in the society and made partakers of His divine nature. "Whereby are given great and precious promises: that by these

ye might be partakers of the divine nature, having escaped the corruption that is in the world through lust." (2 Pet 1:4)

- By faith we walk. Walking in life is not a physical thing, it is spiritual. And to walk right therefore without stumbling, you need faith. "(For we walk by faith, not by sight):" (2 Cor 5:7).

- By faith we are made whole. It is faith that heals, delivers and restores. It is by faith that the works of Satan are destroyed. Without faith, therefore, suffering continues. Hear what the Master had to say to a woman who has been under the yoke of Satan for twelve years, who had suffered several things from many physicians, who has spent all that she had looking for a cure, "Daughter, be of good comfort: thy faith has made thee whole; go in peace." (Lk 8:48, Mt 9:22). Today as you too activate your faith and look up to Jesus for that miracle you have been expecting, I see the Master saying to you, "your faith has delivered it to you, go in peace."

- By faith we overcome. Everyday of our lives is full of challenges, obstacles and conflicts. Faith is the solution. For our victory in any battle of life is dependent on our faith. "For whatsoever is born of God overcometh the world: and this is the victory that overcometh the world, even our faith." (1 Jn 5:4).

- By faith we have access to God. Faith does not only please God, it also grants us access to God. Our prayers, petitions and supplications can only reach God on the vehicle of faith. Faithless intercessions and supplications do not ascend to God. This is why it was said, "In whom we have boldness and access with confidence by the faith of him." (Eph 3:12). This access takes us to His grace wherein we stand; thus the Bible said "By whom also we have access by faith into His grace wherein we stand, and rejoice in hope of glory of God." (Rom 5:2). As you today apply your faith, your entire request shall likewise be granted, and rejoicing shall henceforth be your portion.

- By faith we are united. "Till we all come in the unity of the faith, and of the knowledge of the Son of God, unto a perfect man, unto the measure of the stature of the fullness of Christ." (Eph 4:13). Although this talks mainly of the day of His second coming, faith for the believers is a powerful uniting force. As congregations, families and a church of Jesus, faith unites. Faith in Christ brings people of diverse cultures, languages and colors into a single family – the family of God. And since there is strength in unity, the church becomes a formidable force to reckon with.

- By faith we are shielded. Faith is a shield – a shield from the darts of the wicked one. Without faith, our armour of protection is incomplete. "Wherefore take unto you the whole armour of God, that ye may be able to withstand in the evil day, and having done all, to stand...Above all, taking the shield of faith, wherewith ye shall be able to quench all the fiery darts of the wicked." (Eph 6:13,16). This is a major component of the armour, without it, a hedge will be broken; and remember, "He that diggeth a pit shall fall into it; whoso breaketh a hedge, a serpent shall bite him." (Eccl 10:8).

Therefore run for the cover provided by faith to avoid satanic attacks; and as you do this, I see God protecting and fortifying your defense on regular basis.

The word brings faith.

But faith is not a gift. It is a fruit of the Holy Spirit. It is, therefore, cultivated over a period of time. Faith is a product of the word of God, it cometh by hearing; hearing the word of God. Hear this "So then faith cometh by hearing, and hearing by the word of God." (Rom 10:17).

Faith is not prayed, fasted, cried, meditated or worked for, but it *cometh.* Once the Word is accepted, believed, and confession is made based on the Word that Jesus is the Christ, a measure of this faith is released "as God has dealt to every man a measure of faith." (Rom 12:3). This is the faith that saves and sanctifies. Once this level of faith is obtained, it may either be

- Stagnated and remain as little faith (Mt 6:30). This is very bad and should be fought at all cost. Any one at this level should do everything possible to move forward. What you need to do is very simple. Expose yourself to the word regularly, and your faith will enter into the next level; which is,
- Growing faith (2 Thess 1:3). Faith grows on constant exposure to the word of God, to become,
- Strong faith (Rom 4:20). From here it matures to
- Great faith (Mt 8:10). This is the type of faith that the Bible said could move mountains. With a little more effort, it becomes

- Full faith (Acts 6:5, 11:24), or
- Grounded and settled faith (Col 1:23). However, in the absence of the word, it may become
- Weak faith (Rom 4:19), or even be totally lost leading to a state of
- No faith (Mk 4:40, Deut 32:20, Mt 17:17). This is the same level seen in unbelievers.

The level anyone finds himself is a function of the 'word power' in the person.

True faith.

Different types of faith exist. But in this presentation, we are only talking about the true faith that is, faith authored by, and founded in Jesus (Heb 12:2). This kind of faith may be referred to as the "faith of Jesus" (Rev 14:12), "sincere (unfeigned) faith" (2 Tim 1:5), or "faith of the gospel" (Phil 1:27).

There is only one true faith. Paul testifying to this in Ephesians 4:5, proclaimed that there are only "One Lord, one faith, one baptism."

You may be asking by now, 'what do I have faith in? True faith is real only when, according to Jesus, the Master, it is directed at God. Hear what He said, "Have faith in God." (Mk 11:22).

Only faith in God produces results; and hearing the word of God helps one develop this kind of faith. There is always a great danger when we spend time listening to other things such as the philosophies or doctrines of men. This is because devoting time to hear from other things may result in the development of false forms of faith, and this can destroy a destiny. So, avoid it and hearken to the advice of the scripture. Therefore:

- **"Flee..." (1 Cor 6:18).** Flee from any doctrine that is not of God, and of His Son Jesus Christ.
- **"Submit yourselves therefore to God** (and God only). **Resist the devil, and he will flee from you. Draw nigh to God, and he will draw nigh to you. Cleanse your hands, ye sinners; and purify your hearts, ye double minded." (Jas 4:7-8).**
- **"Be sober, be vigilant** (always, watch out for the devil and all his agents, look out for his tricks and ugly moves)...**whom resist steadfast in the faith." (1 Pet 5:8-9).**
- **"casting down imaginations, and every high thing that exalteth itself against the knowledge of God, and bringing into captivity every thought to the obedience of Christ." (2 Cor. 10:5).**

Faith can fail.

Do you know why you must heed these pieces of advice? The reason is very simple. Faith can fail!

"behold, Satan hath desired to have you, that he may sift you as wheat: But I have prayed for thee, that thy faith fail not:" (Lk 22:31-32). Paul speaking to Timothy, said

"Now the Spirit speaketh expressly, that in the latter times some shall depart from the faith, giving heed to seducing spirits, and doctrines of devils;" (1 Tim 4:1). So faith can fail. Having faith today does not therefore mean that you will have faith all the time. To prevent losing your faith, you must

- **Increase your faith**. Allow it to grow from where it is to either settled or grounded faith levels. Even the disciples of Jesus knew the importance of this, which was why they prayed the Master, saying, "Increase our faith." (Lk 17:5). You too can also desire what they desired today. When they prayed the above prayer, the Master exposed them to more of the word – which is the source of faith. You too can also prayerfully expose yourself to the word by attending more Christian gatherings to hear the word. Remember, faith cometh by hearing the word of God.

- **Contend for your faith**. The devil is all out to steal your joy by making you faithless. He knows that having faith is the only way you can please God. And only God pleasers are overcomers, and only overcomers are kingdom stars. I will, like Apostle Jude, "exhort you that you should earnestly contend for the faith which was once delivered unto the saints." (Jude 3). Like Paul advised Timothy, 'Fight therefore the good fight of faith, that you may lay hold on eternal life'. (1 Tim 6:12). He is also saying to you, 'This charge I commit unto you, therefore, that thou war a good warfare with your faith and all the prophecies that have gone ahead of you'. (1 Tim 1:18).

Your faith is always on trial.

Furthermore, these you must do because your faith is always on trial by the devil and his cohorts. But this is very good for you. Do not be afraid, confused or sad when your faith is tried because I will like to let you know this also, "that the trying of your faith worketh patience." (Jas 1:3). It is therefore good for you when your faith is tried. It is an examination you must pass to climb to next level of faith. Without these trials, you will not excel.

Peter in his attempt to emphasize the need to accept trials, especially those targeted at our faith said,

"That the trail of your faith, being much more precious than of gold that perisheth, though it be tried with fire, might be found unto praise and honour and glory at the appearing of Jesus Christ." (1 Pet 1:7). Thus, it is a good thing when faith is tried. It takes you to a higher level of glory, honour and joy. Above all it enhances your patience, and beautifies your praise.

Beware.

Now let me show you what you must not allow to happen to your faith.

- Do not err from your faith. Do you know that some people have erred from the faith? This may be due to trials or even the love of earthly things.

    "For the love of money is the root of all evil: which while some coveted after, they have erred

from the faith, and pierced themselves through with many sorrows." (1 Tim 6:10).

- Others have denied the faith, maybe due to their actions or inactions, confessions and attitudes. For instance, Paul writing to Timothy said,

"But if any provide not for his own, and specially for those of his own house, he hath denied the faith, and is worse than an infidel." (1 Tim 5:8).

Therefore, I advise you not to deny your faith, for the Master keeps a record. Hear this,

"I know thy works and where thou dwellest, even where Satan's seat is: and thou holdest fast my name, and hast not denied my faith…" (Rev 2:13). I enjoin you, therefore, to keep your faith to the end. This is the easiest access to kingdom excellence that endures to the end of times. And like Paul, when you must have run your race to the end, you can boldly say,

"I have fought a good fight, I have finished my course, I have kept the faith." (2 Tim 4:7).

Do you know that…

Faith is more than a confession? Faith is not just a confession, it is a profession. It is not just what you say, but what you do; for "faith without works *(the Bible said)* is dead." (Jas 2:17,20).

Works serve as the evidence of faith. Where there are no works, faith is dead. See 1 Cor. 15:14; and 1 Thess. 1:3. Remember therefore without ceasing, your works of faith. There are people who think that faith is just a confession. Such people actually make mockery of faith. For instance, it is not unusual to see a sister who is sick, believes that God is able to heal her, and is telling everyone who cares to listen that she is healed, still lying on her bed waiting for pity or sorry from people, and even soliciting and receiving sick person's gifts from people. That is not faith. If faith is at work, the sister would not only confess it, but also will, backed by her faith, live and behave in accordance with her confession. In this case for instance, she would therefore arise and act like someone who has been healed. Then and only then is God committed to making sure that her strength is fully restored. Otherwise, she is only a fake and may never commit God in her situation.

Faith, therefore, expects us to take steps in accordance with what we believe and confess. Where there are no such steps, the faith is dead.

I do know that you already have excellent examples of people who pleased God through faith, and thereby obtained a good report. Most of them are listed out in Hebrews chapter eleven. A good study of Romans Chapter four speaks volume on the faith of Abraham, our covenant father.

However, I will like to tell a story of a woman that really taught me what faith is. She was not listed in the hall of fame of faith giants as documented in Hebrews chapter eleven. The Bible called her the Shunammite woman in 2 Kings Chapter four from verse eight. This woman realized that Elisha was a man of God and showed him a lot of kindness. And because she that receives a prophet because he is a Prophet receives a prophet's reward, she was rewarded adequately. Her barrenness was turned, and she became a joyful mother, even though she did not ask for it.

Then the devil struck! Something unexpected happened from verse nineteen. The boy became sick and died. What did she do? This great woman of faith did not just cry nor sit down to mourn. Neither did she wait for people to show their sympathy for her dead son. Rather, she stood up and took *'faith-full-steps'*.

First, she took the boy into the house and laid him down on the bed Elisha, the prophet, used and shut the door behind him. She did not even tell her husband, or the servants. Then she took an ass and went out in search of the man of God. When her husband accosted her on her strange behaviour and actions, she said, "It shall be well." And when the man of God asked her whether all were well with herself, her husband, and her son; she answered, "It is well."

This was pure faith in action. That is faith with proofs. And because of her faith, her boy was brought back to life.

It is therefore never enough to keep confessing 'it is well'. Take steps like this woman to truly make your situation well indeed. I challenge you today to put motion to your faith, and as you do, God will surprise you by bringing every dead issue around you back to life. This is the energizing key to kingdom excellence.

Faith boosters.

Let me conclude this section by giving you what I consider to be boosters of faith. These boosters are facts that whenever you remember them, you are reassured that God is God. Thus, I will like you to,

✓ Remember that God is never late. He is always on time. All His promises must surely come to pass. "But, beloved, be not ignorant of this one thing, that one day is with the Lord as a thousand years, and a thousand years as one day. The Lord is not slack concerning His promises, as some men count slackness; but is longsuffering to us-ward, not willing that any should perish...But the day of the Lord will come as a thief in the night;" (2 Pet 3:8-10). Your knowledge of this fact, I hope, will help you understand that God's timing is very different from men's timing. So, allow God to do His things at His time. He always makes everything beautiful at His time, not your time. (Eccl 3:11).

✓ Remember also that "the vision is for an appointed time, but at the end it shall speak, and not lie: though it tarry, wait for it; because it will surely come, it will not tarry." (Hab 2:3). Every divinely ordained vision must speak. However, they do speak at their appointed time, not your time. So, allow it to speak at the fullness of time. Just know that none of the words of God that had proceeded out of His mouth shall return to Him void. They must accomplish that for which they were sent. Hear what Isaiah had to say about the plans and purposes of God,

"For my thoughts are not your thoughts, neither are your ways my ways, saith the Lord. For as the heavens are higher than the earth, so are my ways higher than your ways, and my thoughts than your thoughts." (Is 55:8-9). For as the rain comes down from heaven and fulfills its mission on earth, so also will the word of God accomplish that for which it was sent. It shall never return void. (Vs. 10-11). So, relax, allow God to do His things. You will never be disappointed.

Faith is the vehicle to kingdom excellence. It is actually the power back up for kingdom excellence. No one can make it in the kingdom without this component of the fruit of the Spirit. Go for it, cultivate it, protect it, and stand firm in it. When you do this, kingdom excellence becomes a reality in your life.

Therefore, I admonish you, using Paul's words,

"Watch ye, stand fast in the faith, quit you like men, be strong." (1 Cor 16:13).

CHAPTER EIGHTEEN

MEEKNESS

"In humility is honour."

This is a very important key in the fruit of the Spirit. Meekness talks about humility, lowly in heart, a heart that is ready to accept correction and learn. It is a major prerequisite for kingdom excellence and making maximum impact in life. Let us start by looking at some kingdom stars that were very meek.

Moses, an abandoned baby, had the rare privilege to be raised in the palace of Pharaoh, king of Egypt. For the first years of his life, he lived as a prince,. but a time came when he realized who he was and chose to identify with his low and afflicted people. As if this was not enough, he fought like a common street boy, killed an Egyptian, and ran away. While in Midian, he delivered some ladies from the shepherds and helped them water their flocks. This act of kindness made the father of the ladies to invite him into their home, and even allowed him to marry one of his daughters. Then this palace raised boy brought himself very low to be a shepherd unto his father-in-law. Thus, it was recorded,

"Now Moses kept the flock of Jethro his father in law, the priest of Midian and he led the flock to the backside of the desert, and came to the mountain of God, even to Horeb." (Ex 3:1).Despite his palace upbringing, he still brought himself so low as to be a shepherd of flock – not even his own flock – but that of his father in law. No wonder the Bible described him as the meekest man in all the earth.

"Now the man Moses was very meek, above all the men which were upon the face of the earth." (Num 12:3). You know what? It was at this low place that God found him and called him to shepherd an entire nation – Israel – of over 3 million people.

David is another example. He was a kingdom star who rose on the wings of meekness. While Saul's popularity made him proud and arrogant, David remained humble even when the entire nation praised him. Even though God had already chosen him in place of Saul (and has even anointed him via Samuel) and everything he did succeeded, when Saul invited him to lead a battle against the Philistines in exchange for his daughter as wife if he wins, David had this to say,

"Who am I? And what is my life, or my father's family in Israel, that I should be son in law to the king?" (1 Sam 18:18). What a meek man. The most amazing thing about this statement was that he was not pretending. I believe he meant every single word of it.

Jesus is another very good example. He left His throne in heaven to come here on earth to suffer for you and me, Was born by a woman espoused to a carpenter, was delivered in a manger, lived like a nobody for thirty years, was baptized by somebody who confessed that he was not qualified to tie the shoes of Jesus, allowed Himself to be kidnapped, insulted, mocked, rejected, flogged, bruised, and crucified, despite His overwhelming powers and authority. What a man of meekness. Paul talking about Christ wrote,

"Let this mind be in you, which was also in Christ Jesus: Who being in the form of God, thought it not robbery to be equal with God: But made himself of no reputation, and took upon him the form of a servant, and was made in the likeness of men: And being found in the fashion as a man, he humbled himself, and became obedient unto death, even death on the cross." (Phil 2:5-8).

To emphasize the need for every Christian to have this same mind, Christ said,

"Come unto me, all ye that labour and are heavy laden, and I will give you rest. Take my yoke upon you, and learn of me; for I am meek and lowly in heart:" (Mt 11:29). Meekness was therefore the very nature of Christ. No wonder He was an amazement to His generation.

We were told that Peter was seventeen years older than Jesus. But he followed Christ and for three years was calling Jesus 'Master'. He obeyed a man that was young enough to be his son. Imagine what people must have said to him, still he was humble and prompt to minister to this his Master. His attitude made the master to say,

161

"That thou art Peter, and upon this rock I will build my church; and the gates of hell shall not prevail against it." (Mt 16:17). And Peter realizing that his promotion was a product of his meekness said,

"Be clothed with humility: for God resist the proud, and giveth grace to the humble. Humble yourselves therefore under the mighty hand of God, that he may exalt you in due time:" (1 Pet 5:5-6).

Paul is the last example I will site in this section. He was a trained lawyer. Well read, was highly gifted, very popular and very industrious. But he knew this key of kingdom excellence. So, despite his achievements in the kingdom, he had these to say,

"I am the least of the apostles, that am not meet to be called an apostle...But by the grace of God I am what I am:" (1 Cor 15:9-10). Knowing the benefits of meekness, he advised Christians to be meek. Hear what he had to say,

"Let nothing be done through strife or vain glory; but in lowliness of mind let each esteem other better than themselves." (Phil 2:3). He further admonished all believers, saying,

"Serving the Lord with all humility of mind," (Acts 20:19). And in conclusion, he said,

"For I say, through the grace given unto me, to every man that is among you, not to think of himself more highly than he ought to think; but to think soberly," (Rom 12:3). For him, for instance, his achievements were products of the help he obtained from God, so he said, "Having therefore obtained help from God, I continue unto this day," (Acts 26:22).Do you want to avoid pride?

How not to be proud.

All the above people achieved kingdom excellence and made maximum impacts in life through meekness. But how do you go about it? Meekness, as a fruit, must be cultivated. It is not a gift, you seek it.

"Seek ye the Lord, all ye meek of the earth...seek righteousness, seek meekness:" (Zep 2:3).

Knowing what David knew will make your search easier. People wrongly believe that they are something, and thus pride themselves in their accomplishments and achievements. They fail to understand that whatever they have on earth – cars, houses, money, companies, etc. - are just kept in their trust by God for a while. This false belief results in pride and arrogance. But David had a better understanding. Despite his exploits in war, David wrote,

"What is man, that thou art mindful of him? And the son of man, that thou visitest him?" (Ps 8:4).

But in the fallen nature of man, meekness is impossible. Only the regenerated people are capable of producing this fruit. And even at that, it is not an easy fruit to bear. It is of a great price in the sight of God.

"But let it be the hidden man of the heart, in that which is not corruptible, even the ornament of a meek and quiet spirit, which is in the sight of God of great price." (1 Pet 3:4).

Meekness attracts God.

How does meekness procure kingdom excellence and maximum impact in life? Meekness is like a perfume. It attracts God. It tells God that you are ready to be guided and taught, for God is only committed to teach and guide the meek,

"The Spirit of the Lord God is upon me; because the Lord hath anointed me to preach good tidings unto the meek." (Is 61:1). Actually, good tidings are preached only to the meek. It is a requirement from God (Micah 6:8). When God sees that you have fulfilled this important requirement, then he will guide and teach you. Psalm even said so.

"The meek will he guide in judgment: and the meek will he teach his way." (Ps 25:9). When your meekness is therefore certified, God will teach you His ways. Remember, only the trained shall be trusted. Once you are fully trained, the earth is handed over to you as your inheritance. That was why the Master himself said,

"Blessed are the meek: for they shall inherit the earth." (Mt 5:5). And while also emphasizing their relevance in heaven and their rating with God, Jesus said,

"Whosoever therefore shall humble himself this little child, the same is the greatest in the kingdom of heaven." (Mt 18:4).

Watch out.

However, meekness like faith could be tested. God may take you through a journey to see how meek you are (Deut 8:2). There is no calling of God without a test. You only partake in the glory after you have passed the test. The path of meekness is actually the path to His glory.

Meekness as a fruit of the Spirit has several benefits, apart from eventual inheritance of the earth. These benefits towards kingdom excellence include,

- **Removal of shame**. Remember Naaman, the leper. The Bible described him as the captain of the host of the king of Syria, a great man with his master, and honourable through whom the Lord gave deliverance to Syria and a mighty man of valour. However, despite this credential, he had time to listen and adhere to the counsel of 'a little maid' who was brought from Israel as a captive and was made to wait on Naaman's wife. And later, in support to his meek spirit, he listened to his servants when they advised him to adhere to the instructions of Prophet Elisha. By his humility, his shame was wiped away (2 Kings 5:1-14).
- **Aversion of destruction**. Anytime God sees a meek heart, He relaxes His judgment. This happened even in Israel; "And when the Lord saw that they humbled themselves, the word of the Lord came to Shemaiah, saying, they have humbled themselves; therefore I will not destroy them, but I will grant them deliverance;" (2 Chron 12:7). It does not only

avert destructions; it also brings deliverance from the Lord.

- **Freedom from affliction.** Talking about Manasseh, the Bible said, "And when he was in affliction, he besought the Lord his God, and humbled himself greatly before the God of his fathers, And prayed unto him: and he was entreated of him, and heard his supplication, and brought him again..." (2 Chron 33:12-13). This takes us to the next advantage.
- **Accelerated prayer answers**. Like Manasseh, meekness accelerates prayer answers from God. The Psalmist testifying to this said, "He forgetteth not the cry of the humble" (Ps 9:12).
- **Divine provisions**. Remember, the meek, Jesus said, shall inherit the earth – and its fullness. Christ in the above statement was confirming what David and Solomon saw and documented.

"But the meek shall inherit the earth; and shall delight themselves in the abundance of peace." (Ps 37:11). Solomon confirming this benefit of meekness to which his father testified to, said, "By humility and the fear of the Lord are riches, and honour, and life. (Prov 22:4). Thus "the meek shall eat and be satisfied:" (Ps 22:26). Do you, therefore, desire kingdom excellence in the area of prosperity, this is the key. Desire it, seek it, cultivate it, and I see you becoming a wonder to your generation.

- **Meekness procures beauty**. The Lord is in the habit of beautifying the meek with all that pertains to life and godliness. The Psalmist confirmed this too when he said, "For the Lord taketh pleasure in his people: he will beautify the meek with salvation." (Ps 149:4).

• **Honour.** Do you desire honour in life? Meekness is the key. Hear what the wisest man that ever lived had to say, "...before honour is meekness." (Prov 15:33). Honour does not come except on the platform of meekness. No wonder James said, "God resist the proud, but giveth grace to the humble." (Jas 4:6). The honour from the Lord comes only to the humble.

As you cultivate this kingdom key of meekness, I see all the above benefits becoming yours for the asking in the mighty name of Jesus, amen.

This is the key that makes God your daily companion. Without God around you, you can do nothing. So, I beseech you with the love of God to seek and re-seek this fruit until you have it. When God sees your heart, He will put it in your heart.

Let me say here that meekness has nothing to do with the way you look, walk or talk. It is purely a thing of the heart. Therefore "Keep your heart with all diligence; for out of it are the issues of life." (Prov 4:23).

CHAPTER NINETEEN

SELF-CONTROL

"When you see a life devoid of self-control
You have just seen a life doomed to fail."

This is the last fruit of the Spirit mentioned in the anchor scripture in Galatians 5:22-23. Let us go through the scripture again. I hope you have not forgotten it. If you have, let me remind you one more time. The passage said,

"But the fruit of the Spirit is love, joy, peace, longsuffering, gentleness, goodness, faith, meekness, temperance (self-control): against such there is no law."

Self-control is what is referred to as temperance in the above scripture. It is defined as a moderation in action, thought or feeling. Having a restraint mentality!

Temperance is the last, but not the least of these fruits. It is cited last to show how important it is for the full manifestation of the benefits of the fruits of the Spirit.

Over the last few chapters, we have systematically dealt with all the other fruits. Now let us try and do justice to this very important fruit.

What is Self-control?

As stated above, temperance (also known as self-control), talks about the ability to do things in moderation, keep one's feeling in check, adequately managing one's behaviour, refusing to join in a discussion or activity that one considers unproductive, or even saying no when and where necessary. This is the key that tells people what we are.

You are not really what you say you are, rather you are what your character says you are. Many lives today are in crisis because of the near absence of self-control. Most career crisis are actually traceable to character crisis. And this character crisis results usually from poor or lack of self-control.

I, therefore, present to you this vital key that has on one hand helped a lot of people climb to the top; while on the other, when neglected, made a lot of people live in regrets. But regrets shall not be your portion in Jesus name.

This fruit makes all other fruits express themselves fully in any one's life. I, therefore, encourage you to embrace this key, and live a life full of joy, peace, and happiness.

Is self-control a gift?

Self-control, like other fruits, is not a gift. It is a fruit; and as a fruit, it must be cultivated. That is why Peter while advising Christians said,

"Add to your faith virtue; and to virtue knowledge; And to knowledge temperance;" (2 Pet 1:5-6). Did you hear that? Add, not take; add, not collect. This shows that self-control does not just come, you deliberately add it to your other fruits to make a whole bunch.

Benefits of self-control.

Do you desire to be a master in the affairs of life? Then add this all-important component. Hear what Paul had to say concerning it;

"And every man that striveth for mastery is temperate in all things." (1 Cor 9:25). That is, such a person is completely self-controlled. Nothing controls him. He is a master of himself. This shows that to be a master in the things of life, one must, as a prerequisite, be a master of himself – his feelings, tongue, resources, etc. There is no short cut!

What do you need to control?

Let me now show you some areas of your life that tells the whole world how self-controlled you are. These are what you need to control. The list is definitely not exhaustive. You can add other things to it. You do not need to tell anybody that you are temperate. Your attitudes, words and looks do.

To be completely in charge of your life, you must control (and properly too) the following areas (among all others) of your life;

- **Tongue**. Your tongue is a very important organ for kingdom excellence and life impacts. What you say, how you say it, where you say it, and even when you say it matters a lot in the things of the kingdom. I have already talked about the key of confession. However, I will try to prevent unnecessary repetition. James in emphasizing the importance of the tongue said,

"For in many things we offend all. If any man offend not in word, the same is a perfect man, and able also to bridle the whole body." (James 3: 2). Any man who is in total control of his tongue, the Bible said; '...is a perfect man'. And perfection is a requirement for kingdom excellence. Again, the Bible said from where we just read that proper control of the tongue enhances total control of all other parts of the body. Do you know why? What you say determines what you see. What you do not say, therefore, you do not see. Adequate tongue control prevents calamities. This was why the Bible said,

"He that keepeth his mouth keepeth his life: but he that openeth wide his lips shall have destruction." (Prov 13:3).

"A fool's mouth are his destruction, and his lips are the snare of his soul" (Prov 18:7).

"Death and life are in the power of the tongue: and they that love it shall eat the fruit thereof." (Prov 18:21)

"Whoso keepeth his mouth and his tongue keepeth his soul from trouble." (Prov 21:23).

Keeping your mouth, therefore, from speaking guile is the first step towards a problem free life. Keep it. In addition, it procures long life and a life of good things. Hear the advice of the elderly,

"Come, ye children, hearken unto me: I will teach you the fear of the Lord. What man is he that desireth life, and loveth many days, that he may see good? Keep thy tongue from evil, and thy lips from speaking guile." (Ps 34:11-12). Keeping your mouth from evil and your tongue from speaking guile, the Psalmist said, in addition to its' benefits of long and pleasant days, is the fear of the Lord.

The best way to keep your mouth from entrapping you is to hearken to the advice of James, "my beloved brethren, let every man be swift to hear, slow to speak, slow to wrath:" (Jas 1:19).

I will like you to know that only people with controlled lips have a future. If your lips are not controlled, your destiny is lost. Therefore, control your lips and fly into your glorious destiny.

This is because, the greatest obstacles to your destiny is not the devil, nor your enemies, but your mouth. Remember, that the Bible said, "For by thy words thou shalt be justified, and by thy words thou shalt be condemned." (Mt 12:37). Not by the words of your enemies, your adversaries nor devil; but by your own words. No wonder the bible went on to say, "How forcible are right words!" (Job 6:25).

You keep God at work (and sometimes the devil at work too) to the degree of your confessions. Your mouth determines the flow of God's power in your direction. No matter how long you prayed, a single wrong word can completely cancel it.

Your tongue is the commonest cause of trouble for most Christians. They constantly break the hedge by their tongue. And whosoever breaks the hedge, the serpent bites. Therefore, control what you say, how you say it, when you say it, and even where you say it.

Do you know why you must control your tongue to excel? This is because God only shows His salvation to those that are able to control their tongues; even the psalmist said it. Hear what he said, "Whoso offereth praise glorifieth me: and to him that ordereth his conversation aright will I show the salvation of God." (Ps 50:23).

Speak life to your situations, health to your body, and healing to your world. And as you do all these, I see your life become a sign and a wonder to your generation.

- **Sleep**. Another area of your life that needs control is sleep. Sleep is good for everybody. But excess sleep is a destiny destroyer. Hear this,

    "How long wilt thou sleep, O sluggard? When wilt thou arise out of thy sleep. Yet a little sleep, a little slumber, a little folding of the hands to sleep: So shall thy poverty come as one that travelleth, and thy want as an armed man." (Prov 6:9-11). The above scripture was repeated in Proverbs 24:33-34. Why? I believe to make it very clear how important it is to all, and to emphasize the fact the uncontrolled sleep is a destiny destroyer.

Excess sleep does not only bring poverty with it – which for sure it does bring – but also frustrations, depression and sorrow.

I will like to make you understand that sleep here does not only mean lying on bed and closing your eyes. No. It goes beyond that. It includes idling away your time in nothingness, not using your brain for productive ventures, allowing your resources to be wasted in irrelevant things, and other similar time-wasting activities like gossiping.

Avoid sleeping at the wrong time with all your strength. It is a killer. A lazy man cannot achieve kingdom excellence. The topmost top is not meant for sluggards. Kick that bad habit away. Set a goal and pursue it. See you at the top.

- **Time**. Time is a common resource for all. The rich or the poor, the master or the servant, the driver or the tout, the manager or the messenger, all have the same amount of time per day. God has dealt unto everyone the same measure of time – twenty-four hours – everyday. Nobody has an advantage of time over another. However, the difference is on what each person does with his or her time. If you waste your time, you waste your life; when you spend the time, you spend your life; but if you invest your time, you invest into your future. Many spend or even waste their time; very few invest theirs. This is one of the major reasons for the difference in the socio-economic standard of many people.

Again, among the few that invest their time, what they invest their time into also matters. That is why the Bible said,

"but time and chances happen to them all." (Eccl 9:11). What you do with your time determines what becomes of your destiny in life.

Here this, "To everything there is a season, and a time to every purpose under the heaven:" (Eccl 3:1). If you miss the season for your advancement in life, or the time for that purpose of God for your life, you are really in trouble. Work therefore with time. Even God works with time.

Are you surprised? God really works with time. After all, He created the whole earth in six days. Why do you think He had to tell us that the whole earth was created in six days, and that He rested on the seventh day? He could have just stopped at verse one by telling us that in the beginning, God made the heaven and earth. No. He did not stop there. The Bible even told us what He created on each day, and how He spent the rest of the day. That shows that God has a divine program for each day.

Before the floods came, He told us how long it took Noah to build the ark; and when the floods came, He also told us how long it rained, and even how long it took the winds to completely dry the land.

When Abraham went to sacrifice Isaac, the Bible told us how many days it took him to arrive at the altar of sacrifice. The list is endless. God works with time!

What about you? Do you wake up each day and just jump into it without a good idea of what you are supposed to do throughout the day? Then you are bound to waste the time and day. For "Where there is no vision the people perish." (Prov 29:18).

Organize your time, plan your day, work according to your plan, and be realistic in your planning. Even God plans. He planned creation – light came before other things, the sea before the fishes, the herbs before the animals, etc. Remember, when you fail to plan, you invariably plan to fail. But you shall not fail.

In organizing your day, seek God's opinion, for "There are many devices (plans) in a man's heart; nevertheless the counsel of the Lord, that shall stand." (Prov 19:21). So, in order to avoid frustrations, plan your day and activities in accordance to the purpose of God for your life.

Peradventure you do not know this, ask Him. Never start any day without first talking to God. This is the key most kingdom stars are using. When God is involved, divine backing is guaranteed; where God leads, divine supplies are waiting; and if God is involved, oppositions are none issue.

Do you know why time is very important? Every miracle, blessing, or provision from God has a due season. They are yours only "in their due season." (Num 28:2). If you miss it, you may never have the opportunity again to get them.

Some people believe that they have a lot of time. But time waits for no one. Use it while you have it. Even if you are to spend 120 years on earth (Gen 6:3), 120 years is not eternity. If you are 25years now, that means that you have less than 100 years more to live. Do not waste it.

Your 120 years, so to say, is like a handbreadth and that is what the Psalmist said. Hear him, "Behold, thou hast made my days an handbreadth; and my age is as nothing before thee." (Ps 39:5). Therefore "remember how short my (your) time is:" (Ps 89:47), and that "his (your) days are as a shadow that passeth away." (Ps 144:4), and use them well.

- **Eyes**. I will like to talk about your eyes here because this is one organ that has led many to the pit of death – bottomless pit. The eyes are vital for kingdom excellence, but when wrongly used, they can destroy a glorious destiny. They are the primary instrument of lust and immorality. What the eyes do not see, the heart does not desire. So, watch what you see or desire to see.

Every sin committed undergoes a process. With the eyes, the problem cycle begins. But if you are in total control of what you look at, the process will be aborted even before it starts. We are not talking about just seeing something. No. We are referring to spending time to look at it, sometimes several times over; no wonder our Lord Jesus, knowing the vital role the eyes play in immorality said,

"Ye have heard that it was said by them of old time, Thou shall not commit adultery: But I say unto you, That whosoever looketh on a woman to lust after her hath committed adultery with her already in his heart." (Mt 5:28). You may be wondering how this is possible. The eye is the gateway to the brain. So, once the eyes accept it as good, the mind and body systems will start misbehaving.

Remember what happened to Eve in the Garden of Eden. The Bible recorded that "when the woman saw that the tree was good for food, and that it was pleasant to the eyes, and a tree to be desired to make one wise, she took of the tree thereof, and did eat," (Gen 3:6). Notice that the tree has been in the garden all this while. But immediately her eyes took extra notice of it, sin entered. She later blamed the serpent. But hear what the Bible has to say,

"Let no man say when he is tempted, I am tempted of God: for God cannot be tempted with evil, neither tempteth he any man: But every man is tempted, when he is drawn away by his lust, and enticed. Then when lust has conceived, it bringeth forth sin: and sin, when it is finished, bringeth forth death." (Jas 1:13-15). It is your lust that draws you away and entices you, not circumstances. Therefore, watch it.

Be careful what you see and what you pay attention to. The devil uses this avenue a lot. He used it with Eve and it worked, he will still use it again and again.

• **Appetite.** This is another thing you must control. Remember, it is written, "man doth not live by bread only." (Deut 8:3). So, control your appetite. Any person that eats everything that comes his way, everywhere, every time is not a candidate for kingdom excellence.

I see a lot of fat people around these days. But the interesting thing is that most of them never believe that they eat enough, talk less of too much. It is therefore not unusual to hear them say, "I don't know what is wrong with me, I hardly eat anything, but still I keep getting fat." Let me make it clear here that no tree grows without nourishment, no animal increases without food, and similarly, no human cell enlarges or replicates without adequate stimulants.

However, some people may be predisposed to obesity. Such group of people should as a necessity, invest more time in exercise, be more disciplined in their appetite, and watch what they do with their time.

Fasting helps you discipline your appetite – apart from its spiritual benefits. So, do it often. And as you obey these simple but vital instructions, you will soon get to the topmost top.

You can also exercise self-control in your dressing, associations, etc.

CHAPTER TWENTY

HOLY SPIRIT

"I wait on you, Oh sweet Holy Spirit
for your daily sweet instructions."

We have just finished discussing the series on the fruits of the Spirit. I believe God that the excursion has helped you towards arriving at your place in God. However, in this chapter, we will be talking about the Holy Spirit as a key to kingdom excellence. Are you surprised? Please do not be. Apart from the benefits of the fruit of the Spirit, the Holy Spirit has His own ministry. This is what we will be discussing in this section.

The Holy Spirit is the voice of God, and a member of the Trinity. He has always been with God, right from creation.

"In the beginning, God created the heaven and the earth.... And the Spirit of God moved upon the face of the waters" (Gen 1:1-2).

In the Old Testament, the Almighty God dealt with man directly. He spoke to Noah, Abraham, Moses, Joshua, Samuel, etc. In the New Testament, He sent Jesus Christ, who came into the world, lived like a normal mortal, was crucified, buried, resurrected and ascended into heaven; and is sitting today at the right hand of God the Father interceding and mediating on our behalf.

Today, He still works with men, but this time via the Holy Spirit. Thus, the Holy Spirit is our present sure link to God.

Who is the Holy Spirit?

Let me start by saying that the Holy Spirit is not an 'it'. He is a person. He is not a wind, fire, dove, oil nor water. Although all these may be used to represent the Holy Spirit, they are not the Holy Spirit. The Holy Spirit is a person, with full personality profile. He has a will, emotions and can be grieved.

In the above scripture and many other places like Judges 3:10, 11:29, 1 Samuel 10:6, etc., He is called the Spirit of God; in Psalm 51:11 He is called the Holy Spirit; in Zechariah 12:10, He is called the Spirit of grace and of supplication; in Isaiah 4:4, He is called the Spirit of Judgment; in Mathew 10:20 He is called the Spirit of my Father; in Mark 1:8 He is called the Holy Ghost; in John 14:17 He is called the Spirit of truth; in Isaiah 11:2 he is the Spirit of wisdom, understanding, counsel, might, knowledge and of the fear of the Lord; in Romans 8:2, He is called the Spirit of life; in Ephesians 1:13, he is called the Spirit of promise; in 1 Peter 4:14, He is called the Spirit of glory; and in Revelation 19:10 He is called the Spirit of prophecy.

These names and some others that I have not included in this section highlight the various ministries of the Holy Spirit.

Let me also inform you that the Holy Spirit is not a feeling, a sensation nor a myth, He has a voice. This voice can be heard, but by only those that have been redeemed by the precious blood of Jesus. When they hear Him, they obey Him; for the Master said, "My sheep hear my voice, and I know them, and they follow me."(Jn 10:27).

What is the purpose for the Holy Spirit?

God sent the Holy Spirit to all believers for a purpose. And that is to help us maximize destinies and make maximum impact in life. One thing is to be filled with the Holy Spirit, and to speak in other tongues, but it is another thing entirely to benefit from the numerous ministries of the Holy Spirit.

As his names imply, the Holy Spirit is not just for speaking in tongues {although this is a vital function, especially in the area of building up our faith (Tit 20)}, but more importantly He has a duty to make us excel in life and in the kingdom. This is possible because the Holy Spirit is the Spirit of Excellence and is given to us for profiting.

A proper understanding of the ministry of the Holy Spirit is, therefore, very important for maximization of the inherent benefits of this component of the Godhead.

Let me start by saying that the coming of the Holy Spirit is a fulfillment of the promise of God to all His children. A promise He made through Prophet Joel,

"And it shall come to pass afterward, that I will pour out my Spirit upon all flesh; and your sons and daughters shall prophesy, your old men shall dream dreams, your young men shall see visions: And also upon the servants and upon the handmaids in those days will I pour out my Spirit." (Joel 2:28-29).

This promise was fulfilled on Pentecost day. Peter testifying to this on that day, while answering the crowd who thought that they were a bunch of drunken men, reminded them of this prophecy by saying,

"But this is that which was spoken by the prophet Joel; And it shall come to pass in the last days, saith God, I will pour out of my Spirit upon all flesh..." (Acts 2:16-17). This promise had to be fulfilled and urgently too for the Christians to take their rightful place both in God and on earth. Why? In the absence of the fulfillment of this promise, the gospel will not yield the required results. Hear what Isaiah said concerning this,

"Until the Spirit be poured upon us from on high, and the wilderness be a fruitful field, and the fruitful field be counted as a forest." (Is 34:15). In order words, until the Spirit is poured forth upon all believers, the efforts of all people may yield nothing. But once the Spirit is poured forth, every wilderness of life will become a fruitful field – even wilderness that hitherto had refused to yield any fruit – and gradually the wilderness will become a forest. This is the primary mission of the Holy Spirit – to make our faith in God productive and rewarding.

Where is the seat of the Holy Spirit?

The Holy Spirit is not poured anywhere. It has only one dwelling place, and that is the heart of man; more specifically, the heart of a redeemed man.

"Who hath sealed also us, and given the earnest of the Spirit in our hearts." (2 Cor 1:22). No wonder therefore we are advised to guard our hearts diligently, for out of it are the issues of life. (Prov 4:23).

You may be asking, 'when can I get this Holy Spirit, and how?' As for when, you can actually be filled with the Holy Spirit even from your mother's womb. Jesus, for instance was filled while in His mother's womb. The angel that announced His coming said so,

"And He shall be filled with the Holy Ghost, even from his mother's womb." (Lk 1:15). You may say, 'the Bible was talking about the messiah, Jesus. Yes, you are right. But also remember that the messiah Himself said,

"As my Father hath sent me, even so send I you." (Jn 20:21). So, if He came filled with the Holy Ghost right from the Womb, you too can. This is where Christian parents come in. Pray for your babies in the womb. Actually, you are expected to start praying for your babies even before they are conceived in the womb. Decree what you want and for their everlasting love for God. You can even pray for their infilling right from the womb!

But if you are an adult already, it is still not late. You can get filled now as you read this book. This is through what the Bible called the baptism of the Holy Spirit – just like the early Apostles of Jesus.

The baptizer is Jesus Himself (Lk 3:16, Jn 1:33, Acts 1:5) and He can baptize you either,

- Through His word, for His words are Spirit and they are life (Jn 6:63),
- Anointing with a holy oil (1 Sam 16:13),
- Laying on of hands by his servants (Acts 8:17, 19:6),
- Prayers made by anointed men of God, or even by a personal petition to God (Acts 8:15), or
- Through the use of mantles and other mysteries of God.

But this is a prerogative of believers only. Peradventure you are still not born again, getting born-again is the very first step. Do it now.

How?

Confess your sins, repent of them, make a vow not to go back to them and then pray the sinners' prayer on the last page of this book. I will also pray with you!

You have just prayed the sinner's prayer? Congratulations. You are now a new creature, old things have passed away, behold all things have become new. God has cancelled your name from the book of death, and written it into the book of life. You are now qualified for Holy Ghost baptism. Welcome to the true winners' club. It is as simple as that.

Do you know why it is this simple? It is not His desire that any should perish, but that all should come to the knowledge of Him, (2 Pet 3:9). That is why since you were born, He has been at the door of your heart knocking, waiting for a day like this when you will hear and open for Him to come in to dine with you. (Rev 3:20).

Now that you are born again, kneel and pray for the baptism of the Holy Spirit. And as you ask earnestly, I see God filling you up with His presence, amen.

You may say this prayer;

Lord Jesus, thank you for dying for me on the cross of Calvary. Your death and resurrection saved me from the power of sin and death. I am forever very grateful. Before you left this world, Lord, you promised that you would send to us, your sons and daughters, the Holy Spirit, as a comforter who is to teach us all things and bring to our remembrance all the things you did and taught. I desire the baptism of the Holy Spirit. I therefore ask that you baptize me with your Holy Spirit, even right now. Fill me up, make my body your temple, and manifest your presence in my life. I thank you for this new baptism, for I know that my expectations shall not be cut off, and everyone that asks according to your will, you always answer. I ask in the mighty name of our Lord and Saviour, Jesus Christ, amen.

Now believe you have received, open your mouth wide and speak in the language of the Spirit. It is very refreshing!

Benefits of Holy Spirit baptism.

Do you know why you really need Him? Without Him, you are like any other natural common powerless human being; but with Him, you become supernatural; without Him you cannot see beyond your nose, and wonders are far from you; but with Him, you become un-molestable, unchallengeable, and unstoppable, because you are now a spirit, for

"That which is born of the flesh is flesh; and that which is born of the Spirit is spirit." And like a spirit, "The wind bloweth where it listeth, and thou hearest the sound thereof, but canst not tell whence it cometh, and whither it goeth: so is everyone that is born of the Spirit." (Jn 3:6,8). So being filled with the Holy Spirit makes you highly unpredictable to your enemies. They shall see you but cannot reach you; they may even reach out for you but will never be able to catch you. You become a true wonder to them all.

In addition, being born again and filled with the Holy Spirit make you a true worshipper of God. The Bible said,

"But the hour cometh, and now is, when the true worshippers shall worship the Father in spirit and in truth: *(for)* the father seeketh such to worship him. For God is a Spirit; and they that worship Him must worship Him in spirit and in truth." (Jn 4:23-24).

Furthermore, baptism of the Holy Spirit equips you with the required power to do the will and work of God.

"But ye shall receive power, after that the Holy Ghost is come upon you: and ye shall be witnesses unto me both in Jerusalem, and in Judaea, and in Samaria, and unto the uttermost part of the earth." (Acts 1:8). So, the power to become a witness for Christ comes only after (not before) the baptism of the Holy Spirit. This explains the boldness of Peter after the baptism, who before now was hiding from people (including a small girl). You need this power because the race is not to the swift, nor the battle to the strong, neither yet bread to the wise…(Eccl 9:11). The Holy Spirit makes all the difference.

After the baptism, what next?

Now that you are filled, the level of the Holy Spirit in you matters too. You must strive to be full of the Holy Spirit, like Jesus, the author and finisher of our faith (Lk 4:1). That is the only way you can enjoy the maximum benefits of the Holy Spirit. Therefore, I, like Paul, admonish you,

"be not drunk with wine, wherein is excess; but be filled with the Spirit; Speaking to yourselves in psalms and hymns and spiritual songs, singing and making melody in your hearts to the Lord." (Eph 5:18-19).

It is only when you are filled that the Spirit flows out from you, like rivers of living waters (Jn 7:38). And you need a flowing out level to be in charge of your environment.

Now that you have the key, how does He make you a kingdom star? Let us look at the seven-fold ministry of the Holy Spirit to every believer. These are,

1. **He is a teacher:** The Holy Spirit has a teaching ministry. Without Him, we cannot understand the scriptures. John 14:26 said that the Holy Spirit "shall teach you all things, and bring all things to your remembrance, whatsoever I have said unto you." Furthermore, whenever you are at a loss of what to say, "the Holy Ghost shall teach you in the same hour what ye ought to say (Lk 12:12). Thus, when you are at a loss of what to say, or do towards becoming a kingdom star, the Holy Ghost will immediately come to your aid to sort you out. This He does by quickening your understanding, your mind and your brain when you meditate on the word. See Acts 8:26-31 and10: 19.

2. **He is a comforter**: "But the comforter, which is the Holy Ghost, whom the Father will send in my name, he shall teach you all things, and bring all things to your remembrance, whatsoever I have said unto you." (Jn 14:26). Christ promised us the Comforter, because He did not want to leave us comfortless. See John 14:16-18, 15:26, and Isaiah 40:1.

3. **He is a guide**: The Holy Spirit guides us into all truth. That is, He divinely directs us. "Howbeit when he, the Spirit of truth, is come, he will guide you into all truth: for he will not speak of himself; but whatsoever he shall hear, that shall he speak: and he shall show you things to come." (Jn 16:13).

He reveals the truth of the scriptures to every believer; thereby making the scriptures easily understood. He also guides us even in decision-making. Because of this ministry of the Holy Spirit, it restricts our actions and activities. He constantly ministers to us on what

Obinna Ositadimma Oleribe

to do or what not to do, especially towards kingdom excellence and making maximum impacts. It is not unusual to hear people say, "I was in the house when my spirit told me to go to that office, and immediately I got there, the job was waiting for me." That is the Holy Spirit in action.

He even did guide Paul. Paul during one of his missionary trips was about to go into Bithynia, "but the Spirit suffered him not." (Acts 16:7). As he obeyed the Spirit, he had a vision to go over to Macedonia. Today, the Spirit is still guiding God's children. But we have a duty – to listen – and when we hear, to hearken to the Spirit. This is one major route to kingdom excellence.

4. **He is a counselor**: Everyone needs a counselor. And the Holy Spirit is our everlasting counselor, always right, always sure of the result of His advice because He knows the end from the beginning. Isaiah realizing this great ministry of the Holy Spirit, asked, "Who hath directed the Spirit of the Lord,or being his counselor hath taught him?" (Is 40:13).

The Spirit of the Lord knows all things, being the voice of God, therefore, He cannot be taught by any mortal. On regular basis, He is always teaching God's children how to make it without sweats. To emphasize the importance of this ministry, the Bible said, "Without counsel purposes are disappointed: but in the multitude of counselors they are established." (Prov 15:22). Also, "Where no counsel is, the people fall: but in the multitude of counselors there is safety." (Prov 11:14,

24:6). Thus "Every purpose is established by counsel:" (Prov 20:18). Seek therefore the counsel before every step you take, and you will never stumble nor hurt your foot against a stone.

5. **He is a helper**: This is one of the very important ministries of the Holy Spirit to all Christians. For kingdom excellence is "Not by might, nor by power, but by my Spirit, saith the Lord of Hosts." (Zech 4:6). Thus, Paul said, "Likewise the Spirit helpeth our infirmities: for we know not what we should pray for as we ought: but the Spirit itself maketh intercessions for us with groanings which cannot be uttered." (Rom 8:26). The major areas of the help of the Spirit is in praying aright as well as praying for things we may not even know that we ought to pray for.

Man can pray amiss, but the Holy Spirit cannot, because He knows the mind of God. He helps the prayer of saints. He is our greatest intercessor, interceding for us according to the will of God. Engage the Holy Spirit today, and live a stress free life.

Paul even used this help, so he could say, "Having therefore obtained help, I continue to this day."

6. **He is a quickener**. The Holy Spirit quickens our mortal bodies. He makes our mortal bodies to be alive supernaturally. Hear this, "But if the Spirit of him that raised up Jesus from the dead dwells in you, he that raised up Christ from the dead shall also quicken your mortal bodies by the Spirit that dwelleth in you." (Rom 8:11). It is within the power of the Holy Spirit to make

you healthy. If He dwells in you, you have no reason to be sick. As a sick man cannot make maximum impact nor achieve kingdom excellence, I pray this hour that this ministry of the Holy Spirit shall be made manifest even in your life.

7. **He is a protector**. He protects the believer. This He does by pre-warning the spiritually sensitive ones in times of danger. The Holy Spirit warns in many ways – by speaking to us through the word of God, through our conscience, or sometimes talks to us after the event so that we may retrace our steps.

When we embrace these ministries of the Holy Spirit, we enjoy:

- **Rest**. "The Spirit of the Lord caused him to rest." (Is 63:14). The coming of the Spirit of God is synonymous with the coming of rest.
- **Abundance**. Isaiah 32:15 said *(paraphrased)* 'Until the Spirit is poured upon us from on high, the wilderness will not be fruitful, and the non-fruitful field cannot be counted as a forest. To make the wilderness fruitful, pour out the Spirit.' In other words, the coming of the Spirit signifies the coming of abundance.
- **Liberty.** "The Spirit of the Lord God is upon me…to proclaim liberty to the captives, and the opening of prison doors to them that are bound;" (Is 61:1). The Spirit of God is a carrier of liberty anointing.
- **Progress**. "I will pour my Spirit upon thy seed, and my blessings upon thine offspring: And they shall spring up as among the grass, as willows by the

water courses." (Is 44:3-4). The Spirit produces progress and growth.

- **Transformation**. "But we all, with open face beholding as in a glass the glory of the Lord, are changed into the same image from glory to glory, even as by the Spirit of the Lord. (2 Cor 3:18). The Spirit transforms.
- **Executes** the word of God. (Is 34:16). It is only the Spirit of God that can execute the word of God.

Beware of sinning against the Holy Spirit.

Let me inform you, before you become a victim, that there are grave dangers when you sin against the Holy Spirit. Jesus Christ emphasizing this fact said,

"Wherefore I say unto you, All manner of sin and blasphemy shall be forgiven unto men, but the blasphemy against the Holy Ghost shall not be forgiven unto men. And ...whosoever speaketh against the Holy Ghost, it shall not be forgiven him, neither in this world; neither in the world to come." (Mt 12:31-32). Also see Mark 3:28-29 for emphasis.

Like every personality, the Holy Spirit has emotions. Please, in order to obtain the very best from Him, do not

- **Grieve Him**. The Holy Spirit can be grieved. The Bible said, "And grieve not the Holy Spirit of God, whereby ye are sealed unto the day of redemption." (Eph 4:30). Also see Isaiah 63:10-11. Guard against it. Sin for instance, grieves Him.

- **Quench Him**. The Holy Spirit activities can be quenched. Paul advising the early Christians said, "Quench not the Spirit." (1 Thess 5:19). Acting outside the instructions of the scriptures could quench the Spirit.

- **Resist Him**. Resisting the Holy Spirit equals refusing all His ministries. And a life without the Holy Spirit is a life void of God's power and His manifestation. This is because the Holy Spirit is the power of God and can grant divine speed to accomplish several tasks. Every life void of divine direction is full of crisis and problems; and there is no way such a life can attain kingdom excellence or make maximum impact. Until one is therefore baptized into the realm of power through the infilling of the Holy Spirit, struggle continues. I beseech you therefore not to resist the Holy Spirit, like some do. (Acts 7:51). Please don't.

- **Lie to Him**. Any lie to the Holy Spirit is dangerous. It is suicidal to lie to the Holy Spirit (Acts 5:3). He is the mind of God. And knows everything about you. Lying to him is just foolishness. Do not be caught. Lying does not only annoy the Holy Spirit, it also makes you a servant of the devil, the father of all liars. And since the Holy Spirit cannot behold iniquity, He leaves you to the devil. You shall not be a victim.

Understanding the full ministry of the Holy Spirit will catapult you from the low places of the earth into making maximum impact and kingdom excellence.

CHAPTER TWENTY-ONE

ASK

"Until you ask, you may never receive."

To ask generally, means to request for something from someone – a favour, gift, assistance or help. ASK may also be looked at as an acronym for Asking, Seeking and Knocking. That is asking for what you need, seeking for what you have lost or never had, and knocking at doors holding back your divine provisions or keeping you in captivity. This is essentially what is referred to as prayer.

The importance of this key cannot be over emphasized. Speaking on this key, the Master said,

"Ask, and it shall be given you; seek, and ye shall find; knock, and it shall be opened unto you: For everyone that asketh receiveth; and he that seeketh findeth; and to him that knocketh it shall be opened." (Mt 7:7-8).

Why ask?

Many people are living below their levels, suffering untold hardships, meeting obstacles everywhere they turn to; just because they either refuse to ask or do not even know that they are expected to ask.

James saw this and was very worried by it, so he said; "...ye have not, because ye ask not." (James 4:2). Many people are suffering today because they ask not. Nothing comes to the person whose mouth is sealed. Your heavens are closed as long as your mouth remains closed.

You may be saying 'God, my father, is omniscient and, therefore, knows everything including my needs, desires and expectations.' Yes, that is very true - He does know your needs. He knows not only your needs, but also the solution to them too. Even the things you may not know that you need, He also knows. But our God is a perfect *'gentle God'*. He will never intervene until you invite Him into your affairs. Do you know why? He loves you too much to break into your privacy without invitation. The least He will do, which he is still doing, is to "stand at the door *(of your heart),* and Knock:" only those that hear His knock *(voice)* and open for Him are opportune to fellowship with Him. (Rev 3:20).

Hear what he said,

"Call upon me, and I will answer thee, and show thee great and mighty things, which thou knowest not." (Jer 33:3). It is only those that call upon Him that are privileged to be shown great and mighty things, made to understand the secrets of success, and called into the class of those who partake of the mysteries of God. God does not and will never reveal Himself to any and everybody, but to those that desire Him, and who let Him know of their desires, expectations and problems via prayer. So, call on Him today.

The children of Israel were in bondage for more than four hundred years. God saw it, but did nothing, until they called on Him and asked Him to intervene in their situation, and then He arrived, found Moses and said,

"I have surely seen the affliction of my people which are in Egypt, and have heard their cry by reason of their taskmasters; for I know their sorrows; And I am come down to deliver them..." (Ex 3:7-8). Their calling, not their cries, brought Him down. He still hears when you call. Your calling is the only thing that will bring Him down. Do you desire to see Him in your affairs, then call; call today, call now!

What is prayer?

Prayer is not a monologue, a series of complaining, a request session, and bombardments of heavens with personal needs. No. Prayer is communicating with God, a two-way communication, like a telephone discussion with God. It is neither a telegram nor a fax. Not even a voice mail. It is a time of deliberation and reasoning. It is a time to reason with God. Hear what God had to say about prayer.

"Come now, and let us reason together," (Is 1:18). Towards maximum impact and kingdom excellence, this is one key you cannot do without. In true prayer, you must reason with God.

Why do we need to pray?

Prayer is actually not an option for all those desiring kingdom excellence, but a pre-requisite.

1. Jesus demanded that we pray. While speaking to His disciples, he said, "pray ye therefore…And He spake unto …them…that men ought always to pray, and not faint;" (Lk 10:2, 18:1)
2. Prayer brings God near to us, especially in time of trouble (Ps 10:1)
3. Prayer engages divine helps (Ps 54:2-4).
4. God does not only hear prayers, He always answers them (Ps 4:3). Our God is a prayer answering God. God heard the prayers of Zacharias (Lk 1:13), Solomon (2 Chron 7:12), Isaac (Gen 25:21), Hannah (1 Sam 1:10,19), Samson (Judges 16:28-30), Jabez (1 Chron 4:10), Hezekiah (Is 38:2-5), etc. God is still in the process of answering prayers. I see Him answer yours today as you pray aright.

How not to pray!

For prayers to be answered, they must be prayed aright. James said, "Ye ask, and receive not, because ye ask amiss," (Jas 4:3). Prayers are said amiss when

1. The motives are wrong. (Jas 4:3b). For instance, asking God to give you a car just to show off to the world, or even a particular type of car so that people will know that you have arrived is wrong and may never be answered. Why? Because this is a wrong motive. Asking for a car is not wrong, but having

the above as your motive is wrong. God does not answer such prayers.

2. You are not right with God. Only the righteous is permitted to pray to God; for the prayer of a sinner is an abomination before God. (Prov 15:8; 28:9). God hears only the prayers of His people (Ps 4:3). Here this, "But your iniquities have separated between you and your God, and your sins have hid His face from you, that He will not hear you." (Is 59:2).

   Thus to the sinners, God is saying, "when you spread forth your hands, I will hide my eyes from you: yea, when ye make many prayers, I will not hear: your hands are full of blood." (Is 1:15).

   Do you not know that, "The Lord is far from the wicked: but He heareth *(only)* the prayer of the righteous." (Prov 15:29).

3. Your prayer is not heart felt (Jas 5:16). God only answers prayers that proceed from the heart.

4. Your prayer is not backed by His words. God responds only to His words, He honours His word. So if your prayer does not remind Him of what He said, it is amiss. He said, "Put me in remembrance: let us plead together: declare thou, that thou mayest be justified." (Is 43:26).

5. Your prayers are not backed with facts and reasons. He said, **"Produce your cause, saith the Lord; bring forth your strong reasons, saith the King of Jacob." (Is 41:21).**

How to pray!

To pray aright, therefore, it is advisable that you

6. Pray in your closet (Mt 6:5-6). Prayer is a private communication with God. This does not mean that you should not pray in public, rather at all times and in all places, while praying, let God and God alone be your focus. Once your motive and focus are right, you can "pray everywhere, lifting up holy hands, without wrath and doubting." (1 Tim 2:8).

7. Avoid vain repetitions (Mt 6:7-8). Ask believing, because, "If thou canst believe, all things are possible to him that believeth. (Mk 9:23).

8. Ask in faith. Anything done outside faith is sin, therefore without faith; it is impossible to please God. So "ask in faith, not wavering. For him that wavereth is like a wave of the sea driven with the wind and tossed." (Jas 1:6).

9. Pray without ceasing (1 Thess 5:17). David speaking on the importance of ceaseless prayers said, "Evening, and morning, and at noon, will I pray, and cry aloud: and he shall hear my voice." (Ps 55:17). In addition,

10. Ask in His name. Seal all prayer with the name of Jesus. For Jesus speaking to us said, "If you ask anything in my name, I will do it." (Jn 14:14).

11. Come boldly to God in prayers, not fearful but with a sound mind. (Heb 4:16). For God hath not given us the spirit of fear; but of power, and of love and of a sound mind." (2 Tim 1:7)

12. Pray fervently. Only heart felt prayers are effective. (Jas 5:16).

13. Pray following the example Jesus gave in Mathew 6:9-13. You may also pray beginning with Adoration to the King of kings, then Confess your sins to Him, Thank Him for what He has done already and what He has promised to do which you are yet to touch physically. Then conclude with your Supplications. This is referred to as the ACTS of prayer.

Prayer is a major key to kingdom excellence. There are actually some obstacles to excellence that cannot be surmounted except through prayers. The Master testifying to this said, "This kind can come forth by nothing, but by prayer and fasting." (Mk 9:29).

Therefore, no matter the type of problem, be not anxious. But by prayer, present it to God. For instance, many people ask me, 'what is the treatment or solution to stress?' I refer them to this passage in Philippians, which said, "Be careful for nothing; but in everything by prayer and supplication with thanksgiving let your request be made known unto God." (Phil 4:6). This kind of request produces the peace of God which the Bible said 'passeth all understanding'.

What to pray for,

If you are a new Christian, you may think that your prayers must be centered on you and you alone. No. You may be asking me now, 'who and what then should I pray for?' The bible gave us the answer to the above question. Thus according to the scriptures, we are enjoined to pray for

- All men. Paul speaking on this said, "I exhort therefore, that, first of all, supplications, prayers, intercessions, and giving of thanks, be made for all men;" (1 Tim 2:1).
- Kings, and for all those that are in authority. (1 Tim 2:2). If you desire anything good from your leaders, then pray for them, for, "The king's heart is in the hand of the Lord, as the rivers of water: he turneth it whithersoever he will." (Prov 21:1).
- Men of God. (1 Thess 5:25, 2 Thess 3:1). To excel in the kingdom, you cannot afford not to pray for your ministers of God, for the anointing of God flows like water, from the head downwards (Ps 133:1-3). It is therefore only what the head has that is impacted on the congregation. If therefore you want to excel, always pray for your Pastors.
- For one another. James speaking on this said, "Confess your faults one to another, and pray one for another, that ye may be healed." (Jas 5:16). Praying for one another helps to build up the body of Christ. Moreover, it turns captivity around. The case of Job was a good example. The Bible said concerning Job, "And the Lord turned the captivity of Job, when he prayed for his friends: also the Lord gave Job twice as much as he had before." (Job 42:10).

Great men in the Bible made it through prayers. Men like Samuel (1 Sam 12:23), Nehemiah (Neh 2:4, 4:9), Daniel (Dan 2:16-23, 6:10), Jonah (Jon 2:1-10), Jesus Christ (Mt 14:23, Mk 1:35, 14:35-36, Lk 5:16, 6:12, Jn 17:1-26), the Apostles (Acts 1:4, 3:1, 4:24-30, 12:5), Paul (Rom 1:9-10, Phil1: 4), etc. Having seen all these examples, you have no reason but to do what they did, to obtain what they obtained. Therefore, if kingdom excellence is your destination, prayer is the link.

What is the confidence that we have?

He always answers our prayer as long as we ask according to His will. For "this is the confidence that we have in him, that, if we ask anything according to his will, he heareth us:" (1 Jn 5:14).

So always pray like David prayed and I see you obtain the kinds of result He obtained. Remember, *God does not see your tears, He hears your cry*. Cry today to Him now!

CHAPTER TWENTY-TWO

KINGDOM SERVICE

"What are the things that makes you a kingdom star?
Service, Service, and Service."

We are all made by God. But God does not reckon with all of us. He reckons with only those that are relevant to Him. This is the mystery of relevance.

Look at yourself. Ask yourself this simple question; 'Are you relevant to God?'

In this chapter I will be discussing kingdom service as a master key to kingdom excellence. All other keys are important; but this key is the master key. Take it very seriously. If all along, you have been reading this book as a novel, repent now, and take this aspect very seriously.

Pause and ponder on this.

I know that you come from a family with parents and maybe siblings. Maybe you even have your own family. I will like to take you back memory lane. In your family, who do you associate with, who do you spend your time with regularly, and who do you shower with gifts and blessings? Anybody? No way.

You pay more attention to your parents because from them came your daily sustenance. You may also pay attention to that one or more of your uncles, aunts, sisters or brothers who pay your bills, or who assist you with your daily challenges. Anyone that is useless to you, is either completely avoided or just tolerated. Am I right?

So is God. We are of the family of God – I mean all those that have given their lives to God. God is the head of the family. He loves to see and help those who are relevant to His kingdom. Those that are mere liabilities, He only tolerates.

If kingdom excellence is your goal, you need God's help. Let me show you the easiest way of obtaining this much-needed help. It is the way of service - kingdom service. So, meditate, and make up your mind to be involved, and then God will be involved in your own affairs.

God does not reckon with titles; He reckons with inputs and outcomes. He does not reckon with positions, but usefulness. Your service is your input into the advancement of God's kingdom here on earth. If you have nothing to offer God, He offers you nothing in return. Prayer, fasting and self-chastisements cannot and will never replace kingdom service.

Your service is a seed into the kingdom. If you sow no seed, you reap nothing in reward.

What is kingdom service?

Let me start by saying what it is not. Kingdom service is not the same as worship. Going to church on Sundays to worship God is not kingdom service. I have to say this because many people have been led astray by this lie of the devil that when they go to church on service days, they are serving God. That is not true. Actually, people go to church on service days to obtain from God – be it deliverance, provisions, protection, peace, joy, happiness, etc. So it is not what I mean by service.

Kingdom service is not also being a member of several service groups and being useless in all. No. Kingdom service is taking the kingdom of God as your father's work, becoming committed and relevant to the stones of the kingdom, seeing to the expansion of the kingdom; sacrificing what God has blessed you with, for the growth and expansion of His kingdom.

Service is, therefore, stepping out for God, dedicating your time and other resources for the work of God, deliberately denying yourself of certain life pleasures for the sake of the kingdom of God, giving God back part of what He has blessed you with. This is service! Service is another word for doing all that God has commanded us to do without grumbling, murmurings nor complaining'. (Num. 15:39).

Kingdom service is not one of the options to kingdom excellence. It is the main option. It is not optional; it is mandatory for all those aspiring for kingdom excellence.

Why service?

As long as you are not ready to serve God, the enemy is free to deal with you anyhow it wishes. This is because you are useless, so to say, to God. God has completely nothing to lose with your death, so why worry about you or why waste His resources keeping you alive. Look at the Israelites. Their suffering in Egypt would have continued till eternity, if not that they desired to serve God. God saw their afflictions, their sorrows and the wickedness of their taskmasters, and did nothing. But when He heard their cry for help to free them so that they could be free to serve Him, He came down. And among the very first instructions He gave to Moses were,

"When thou hast brought forth the people out of Egypt, ye shall serve God upon this mountain."(Ex 3:12). This shows the emphasis God places on service.

Look at another case. Hezekiah was sick unto death. He knew that death was at hand. Actually, he had few moments to live by virtue of his illness, which the Bible said was "unto death." Then Isaiah came to confirm what he already knew, by saying,

"Thus saith the Lord, Set thine house in order: for thou shall die, and not live." (Is. 38:1). Isaiah was very right; the chapter on Hezekiah was about to be closed. Then Hezekiah remembered. He remembered that he was not a liability to God, that he was very relevant to the course of the kingdom of God. After all, the Bible recorded that he did that which was right in the sight of the Lord.

What were these things that were right in the sight of the Lord that he did? When he became the Head of State of Israel, he did not waste time to restore the supremacy of God in Israel after his installation. In the first year of his reign, in the first month, he opened the doors of the house of the Lord, and repaired them, sanctified the house and priests of God, destroyed the alters of Baal, removed the high places, broke down the graven images, cut down the groves, and destroyed every idol the people were worshiping. Then he reinstated the Passover feast and restored the worship of the God of their fathers. (2 Kgs 18:1-4, 2 Chron 29, 30, 31). No wonder he could pray to God and said,

"Remember now..." (Is 38:3). And God remembered his works and gave him extra years. In God's book of records, what is there for Him to remember you for? This is the whole essence of service - to provide God with evidence that we are not just liabilities, but useful vessels for His kingdom. Hear what David said,

"The Lord hear thee in the day of trouble; the name of the God of Jacob defend thee; Send thee help from the sanctuary, and strengthen thee out of Zion; Remember all thy offerings, and accept thy burnt sacrifice *(services);*" (Ps 20:1-3). There is a record in heaven. You better write something down now through your service to God.

Are all services acceptable to God?

No. God does not accept all services. There are special requirements which every service must fulfill before it is acceptable before God. God only accepts services that,

❖ **Come out of a willing heart**. God does not force people to serve Him. So only services from a willing heart are accepted. (Eph 6:7, 2 Cor 8:2-5, 12; Ex 35:21)

❖ **Come from a joyful and cheerful heart**. (2 Cor 9:6-8, Deut 28:47-48). As we said earlier, a joyful environment is a God attracting environment. Where there is joy, there is divine presence. Without joy therefore, God cannot be present, and when God is absent, services are neither seen nor accepted.

❖ **Are prompt.** Any service that is not prompt is a waste of time. God works with time. For your obedience to His request for service to be complete, it must be prompt. See a good example in Abraham. When God called him, he departed; when He asked Abraham to sacrifice his son, Abraham did not consult anybody, but obeyed and took steps to fulfill the request early the next morning; and when he was commanded to circumcise all male children including himself, he did not waste any time despite the fact that he was ninety nine years old (Gen 12:3, 17:23-24, 22:3). In all the above situations he acted promptly. That is what God loves. No wonder he is called a friend of God.

❖ **Are total**. Kingdom service is an all or nothing affair. Here, half bread is not better than none. You either give it your all, or you keep it to yourself. God does not reckon with incomplete nor insincere services. I hope you have not forgotten Ananias and Sapphira. While the land was unsold, it was theirs. Even after selling it, the proceeds were still theirs, but to bring a part of the proceed to God and make it look like all, that was totally unacceptable. So, they paid the supreme price (Acts 5:1-10). God is a jealous God. It is either all or nothing. Be warned.

❖ **Are based on our individual abilities**. God knows our capabilities and will therefore not expect us to give what we do not have. In the same vain, He will not accept services that are below our capabilities. Hear what he told Gideon, "Go in this thy might, and thou shall save Israel…" (Judges 6:14). God knows your ability. Jesus also demonstrated this when He gave the parable of the servants whose master was going in a journey and distributed talents to them, "to every man according to his several abilities." (Mt 25:15). Do not therefore deprive yourself of your blessings by offering services that is not commensurate with your ability. Remember, it is either total or nothing. God always weigh actions (1 Sam 2:3).

❖ **Are offered in meekness**. God resists the proud, the Bible said, but giveth grace to the humble. Meekness is a major prerequisite for acceptable service. Paul speaking on this said, "Let nothing be done through strife or vainglory; but in lowliness of mind let each esteem other better than themselves." (Phil 2:3). When you serve God in this way, you shall be exalted just as Christ was exalted. (see verses 5-11).

❖ **Are offered in newness of spirit**, and not in the oldness of the letter. (Rom 7:6).

And to provide the kind of services that please God, you must in addition, be;

❖ **Determined**. In determination, your 'mind is made up never to be deterred' by obstacles, challenges, or trials. Like Solomon, you must be fully determined to give it your very best. (2 Chron 2:1). Proposing to serve God does not bring any reward. What produces reward is the actual service itself. Also see how Daniel determined not to defile himself by eating of the king's meat. (Dan. 1:8). At the end of the day, he was exalted. Determination is the key to glory.

❖ **Dedicated**. Dedication talks about 'deadly commitment' to the things of God. You must be as determined like David and commit yourself dangerously to the things of God. Here him, "Now I have prepared with all my might for the house of my God...Moreover, because I have set my affection to the house of my God, I have of mine own proper good...given to the house of my God, over and above all..." (2 Chron 29:2-5). No wonder God still boasts about him and could boldly declare, "I have found David my servant..." (Ps 89:20). Dedication precedes declaration, deliverance and decoration. God is so willing to boast about you, but He needs to see your dedication first. Also flip back to Job 1:8 and see what God had to say concerning another man who was deadly committed to the things of God.

❖ **Diligent**. Diligence simply means 'delighting in hard work', being dutiful, earnest and consistent. Apart from the fact that God expects us to be diligent in serving Him, diligence in service also distinguishes us, brings honour, power, riches, favour, prosperity and recognition.

Hear these sayings of the wise; "the hand of the diligent maketh rich." "He that diligently seeketh good procureth favour:" "the hand of the diligent shall bear rule:" "the soul of the diligent shall be made fat." And "Seest thou a man diligent in his business? He shall stand before kings; he shall not stand before mean men." (Prov. 10:4, 11:27, 12:24, 13:4, and 22:29). If not for space and time, I would have discussed diligence as a separate key to kingdom excellence. I enjoin you to be diligent in your service to God and see how God Himself will make you to flourish all round.

❖ **Disciplined**. Kingdom stars are highly disciplined people. Indiscipline is a major hindrance to kingdom excellence. Be disciplined in your

- *Associations* (Prov 13:20, 27:17, Eccl 10:10). Iron sharpeneth iron, walking with the wise makes you wise, but companioning with the fools, destroys you. Moreover, be not deceived, evil communications corrupt good manners (1 Cor 15:33). Be wise. Remember, wisdom is profitable to direct.
- *Tongue* (Prov 13:2-3, 25:11,Eccl 5:6). I have previously spoken about your tongue in self-control. Let me remind you that your mouth always creates your world. The world in which you are living now is what you created with your mouth yesterday; and your world tomorrow is dependent on what you say today. When you use your tongue wrongly, you enter into a curse.

Apart from creating your world, your tongue also compels angelic and demonic compliance. Be careful not to use your mouth to destroy your future. Control therefore what you say or do not say.

- *Finances* (Prov 6:6-7, 8:12). Handle your finances with prudence. God expects you to be careful with the resources He has given to you. First, you must appreciate your source to remain resourceful; then you must as a necessity avoid wasting your resources, otherwise the Master will stop the flow. God hates waste. Be very careful. If you desire to have a continuous flow, then be disciplined.
- *Time* (Eccl 3). God is very time conscious, and so must you.
- *Thoughts* (Eph 3:20). Your thoughts are a major key to your future, for as a man thinketh so is he. Think right. Always control what you think about. This is wisdom.
- *Actions* (Jos 1:8, Is 12:3). I do not want to repeat what I said in self-control. God always weighs actions. Watch out.

Having told you a few of the areas you need to discipline, please do yourself a favour, open your book of life and meditate on these passages; and as you do, God will help you bring under subjugation whatever area of your life that needs adequate control.

❖ **Discrete**. God expects you to be discrete in your activities as a servant of God. Remember, "Discretion will preserve thee, understanding shall keep thee." (Prov 2:11). Discretion is a preservative. If you want to stay long enough to enjoy your exalted state in God, then be discrete.

Therefore heed unto the advice of Solomon, "keep sound wisdom and discretion:" (Prov 3:21) and watch out for the seven things that God said He hates in Proverb 6:16-19, which are a proud look, a lying tongue, a hand that shed innocent blood, an heart that deviseth wicked imaginations, feet that be swift in running to mischief, a false witness that speaketh lies, and he that soweth discord among brethren.

❖ **Orderly**. Finally, God expects you to be orderly in the service of God. Disorderliness is not godly. Do not break ranks. Our God loves order in everything. Look at the firmaments, they are still maintaining the instructions given to them at creation, the sun takes care of the day while the moon takes care of the night. The stars are still at their various positions. God truly loves order. Be orderly, and let your service "be done decently and in order." (1 Cor 14:40).

Let us continue in the next chapter by discussing the avenues and benefits of kingdom service.

CHAPTER TWENTY-THREE

KINGDOM SERVICE (PART 2)

"When you serve God, He services your life."

Have you just noticed something? See, service is the very first key that has entered into a second chapter. Does that tell you anything at all?

Service is the gateway to all divine helps. It attracts divine assistance, which is very important in the race of life. Service is not one of the keys to kingdom excellence, it *is* the key; it is not a prerequisite, it is *the* prerequisite for kingdom excellence. Many other keys may be employed, but they will never yield the full result. Understanding this fact will help make your commitment to kingdom service better and your services more acceptable and profitable.

In the last chapter, we tried to emphasize the need for kingdom service.

How can one serve God? To those that are fully persuaded, serving God is a daily delight. I will like you to understand that 'God is not a taskmaster, rather He is a rewarder of them that diligently seek and serve Him; You cannot serve God and decrease, rather you always increase; and as you serve Him, he services your life, destiny and future.' He is not out to hurt you, but to make you. Therefore, embrace service and I see God making you a pride and an envy of your generation.

What are the avenues for kingdom service?

Having said all these let me show you the avenues for kingdom service. You can serve God spiritually, physically and/or materially. Avenues by which you could serve God include;

a. **Prayers.** Praying for the church of God, His ministers, the expansion of the kingdom of God, other people, etc. is one of the avenues of service to the kingdom. This is a spiritual service. Only immature Christians always pray just for themselves. Mature Christians, who are those qualified for kingdom excellence, pray for others too. You are expected to stand in the gap for the sick, the widows, the destitute, the jobless, the barren, the depressed, the afflicted, the pregnant women, the oppressed, etc. Job was afflicted for several chapters of the Bible. Initially, he thought it was God that afflicted him. Later he asked God to show him that which he seeth not, and teach him that which he knew not. Still his affliction continued. But the moment he decided to pray for his friends, "the Lord turned the captivity of Job, when he prayed for his friends: also the Lord gave twice as much as he had before." (Job 42:10). He had a change of status and a restoration of all that the devil took away from him, simply by praying for his friends. Spiritual service is the easiest means for deliverance and restoration. Embrace it today. You can enhance the effectiveness of your prayers by coupling it with fasting and other sacrifices for the growth of His kingdom.

b. **Time.** Devoting your time to the things of God is another avenue of service. This you may do by being a member of a service group like evangelism, choir, sanctuary cleaners, ushers, etc. You must devote a particular time to work for God. Excuses on why you cannot serve God in one capacity or the other excuses you from God's blessings.

c. **Helping other believers.** Maybe you are one of those people God has blessed with a good position, office or job. God expects you to use your good office to help fellow believers, help the move of His kingdom, assist in the spread of the gospel, and even draw fellow highly placed officers to the house of God. This is the main reason why God put you there. If you fail to serve Him with your position, He will remove you and give your place to another person. May no other person take your position as you decide today to work for God even with your office.

d. **Giving.** You are supposed to serve God with your substance. Something must be going out from you on a regular basis to God and His kingdom. David in the example given in the previous chapter served the Lord with his substance while preparing for the building of the temple. This key is vital for supernatural prosperity.

Prayer is a wrong key for financial breakthrough. It cannot solve the problem of poverty. However, the practice of the covenant of giving excuses you from poverty. You can give directly for kingdom expansion like David, to ministers of God like the widow of Zarephath (1 Kgs 17:8-16), to the poor, fatherless and widows like Job (Job 29: 12-16), or to your parents like Jacob (Gen 27: 1-29).

I will talk more on giving in the next chapter while discussing the key of tithe and offering.

Kingdom service is profitable.

Having discussed elaborately the avenues of service, let me now show you how kingdom service procures kingdom excellence; this is what I call the benefits of service.

There is a book of records in heaven. Anytime you serve God, God records it in your name. Once your service pleases Him, he does not say 'thank you' like men do, rather he blesses you. And anytime he blesses, everything works. When everything works for you, kingdom excellence becomes a reality in your life. Hear this,

"And ye shall serve the Lord your God, and He shall bless thy bread, and thy waters; and I will take sicknesses away from the midst of thee. There shall nothing cast their young, nor be barren, in thy land: the number of thy days I will fulfill. I will send my fear before thee, and will destroy all the people to whom thou shall come, and I will make all thine enemies turn their backs unto thee." (Ex 23:25-27). From this passage, kingdom service guarantees,

1. **A hunger free life**. The Lord Himself will bless your bread and your waters. In other words, He will make sure that what to eat, wear or where to live is never a problem to you. When He blesses your bread and waters, they become medicinal to you. Even when you eat any poisonous food, they will not hurt you. The poisons will turn to a vitamin. The Psalmist said, "The young lions do lack, and suffer hunger: but they that seek (serve) the Lord shall not want any good thing." (Ps 34:10). So even when strength fails, they that serve the Lord shall be divinely supplied. Do you remember Joseph? Because he served God and through his service pleased God, he became a Prime Minister in a strange land. Even when all failed, he was in control of the bread of the land. Only healthy and well-fed men get to the top. So, embrace service to obtain strength for the journey.

2. **A disease free life**. He said that He would personally take away sicknesses and diseases from the midst of those that serve Him. No wonder all our covenant fathers were very strong people. Look at Abraham, at eighty years he led a battalion of soldiers to a battle. Caleb also performed a similar feat at about eighty-five years of age. Moses, the Bible recorded "was an hundred and twenty years old when he died: his eyes was not dim, nor his natural strength abated." (Deut 34:7). When you serve God, God becomes committed to your physical welfare and

well-being. Since he loves your service and He needs you healthy to serve Him, He does everything possible to keep you healthy.

To keep you healthy, he becomes your personal physician, prunes you by removing any and everything that will hinder your services to him, and makes sure that at all times you are fit to serve Him (Jn 15:1-5). Do you want God to be your doctor? Then serve Him.

3. **A fruitful and productive life**. He promised to all that serve Him that "none shall cast their young nor be barren." When you serve God, everything works. You become productive in your body, in your business, and in the works of your hand. Even your mind becomes very productive. You become a wonder and a sign to your generation.

   Service secures your works from stagnation, untimely deaths, and failures, makes your works result producing. Service makes your marriage productive and fruitful in all areas of life. Since productivity is therefore an essential requirement for kingdom excellence, you need service to benefit from it.

4. **A productive long life**. He fulfills the number of days of all those that serve Him. After all, the longer you stay, the longer you serve Him, so He keeps you to serve Him more. Remember Hezekiah, when he turned to God in prayer and challenged God with his credentials of service, God gave him fifteen

more years (Is 38:2-5). When God keeps you to serve Him, He also adds blessings, making your stay pleasurable. Hear this, "If they obey and serve him, they shall spend their days in prosperity, and their years in pleasures." (Job 36:11).

In addition, you will not live a fruitless long life, rather, in order to show that the Lord is upright and that there is no unrighteousness in Him, the Bible said, "They shall bring forth fruit in old age; they shall be fat and flourishing;" (Ps 92:14-15).

5. **Divine security**. God protects all those that serve Him. He does this, not for your sake, but for his own sake – to keep you serving Him and to protect His blessings in your life. So, He sends His fear to the camp of your enemies, avenges any disobedience against you, makes all your enemies to turn their backs from you and even destroys any that refuses to leave you alone. He does all these to keep your mind focused and fixed in worshipping Him. Nobody serves God for naught. His service produces a divine hedge round about you, your family, your loved ones and everything you have on every side. Hear what the devil said concerning Job, "Doth Job serve you for naught? Hast not thou made a hedge about him, and about his house, and about all that he hath on every side? Thou hast blessed the works of his hands, and his substance in the land." (Job 1:9-10). God defends all those that serve Him. I see God building a hedge of protection round about you now.

6. **Accelerated prayer life**. Prayers are sweet when answers are guaranteed. Service is a major key to answered prayers. Remember Hezekiah again, God answered quickly and averted a major disaster because he rendered service to God. God answered Hannah's prayer when she vowed to serve Him through the child that would be born, God answered Zachariah's prayer while he was in the temple serving God (Lk 1:11-14). The list is endless. God has not changed; He is still the same yesterday, today and forever (Heb 13:8). For those who have a record with God, when they call, the Lord remembering their services hears them (Ps 20:1-3). However, there are others who due to their exceptional walk with God, do not even need to call before God answers. The choice is yours. As you choose to serve God diligently, I see you become a manifestation of His blessings to your world.

7. **Generational blessings**. When you serve God, God does not only bless you, He also blesses your generation up to the fourth. See what the Lord said unto a man named Jehu that served Him, "Because thou hast done well in executing that which is right in mine eyes…thy children of the fourth generation shall sit on the throne of Israel." (2 Kgs 10:30). Do you like these blessings? Then serve Him.

You must hear this!

There is something you must understand. Kingdom service does not only bring blessings, it also elicits envy. God's overwhelming blessings on the one that truly serves

Him causes people to be envious of that person. These numerous blessings that accrue to these people activate the envy of Satan and all his angels. Be ready to face challenges from your friends, associates, and even family members. When challenges and persecutions arise, "Blessed are ye...Rejoice and be exceedingly glad: for great is your reward in heaven." (Mt 5:11-12).

I will not leave you ignorant of the fact that until your services enkindle persecutions and insults; you are not qualified for great reward. Go therefore all out for God, and I see kingdom excellence becoming a reality for you.

In closing, I will like to take you to Joshua 24:14-15. Hear what it said,"Now therefore fear the Lord, and serve Him in sincerity and truth...serve ye the Lord. And if it seems evil unto you to serve the Lord, choose you this day whom ye will serve...but as for me and my house, we will serve the Lord."

I therefore enjoin you to choose to serve God, for this is the only thing that is needful, which shall not be taken away from you (Lk 10:42).

INTERLUDE

EXCELLENT WISDOM

These are wise sayings. Understanding them will make your walk with God easier, and will help you achieve kingdom excellence without sweats

- ❖ When you are completely sold out for God, God will completely sell everything to your favour.
- ❖ When you give God all you have, He invests His power, wealth and resources in you.
- ❖ If you are fanatic about the things of God, God will be fanatic concerning your welfare.
- ❖ When you fanatically search for God, God will fanatically settle you.
- ❖ When you make God your concern, He takes all your concerns off your shoulder.
- ❖ When you are a slave for God, God makes you a free man on earth.
- ❖ When you are a servant to God, He makes you a master to Satan.
- ❖ When you live for Christ, you die to sin.

- ❖ Your offerings, tithes and sacrifices are loan to God with un-quantifiable interest and un-challengeable returns.
- ❖ If you help the poor, you lend to God.
- ❖ When you promote God's work, He polishes your destiny.
- ❖ When you stand for God, his blessings stand you out.
- ❖ When you sit on His promises, He sits upon your adversaries.
- ❖ As long as you rest on Him, He gives you rest round about.
- ❖ God lovers are kingdom celebrities.

PART FOUR

PROSPERITY KEYS

"Poverty pollutes
Prosperity protects."

Prosperity is of God. It is also Godly to be very rich. I need to say these because over the years the devil had deceived a lot of Christians, and made them to believe that prosperity is ungodly, anti-covenant and worldly. This is a deceitful lie of the devil.

God is holy and righteous. I know you completely agree with that. He is also the richest. Or have you not heard,

"For every beast of the forest is mine, and the cattle upon a thousand hills. If I were hungry, I would not tell thee: for the world is mine, and the fullness thereof." (Ps 50:10, 12). Will you call a God that has such great possessions – the whole earth, the cattle and beasts in the forest, the gold and diamond mines, the wells of crude oils, and every other resource above, within and under the earth - a poor God? No. Even the streets of His kingdom are tarred with gold. (Rev 20:20). But have these made Him an unholy God? No.

These great possessions are actually referred to as God's riches. Hear what the Psalmist said,

"O Lord, how manifold are thy works! In wisdom hast thou made them all: the earth is full of thy riches." (Ps 104:24). He made them, and they were made in wisdom. If the most holy God made them in His wisdom, how can you say that they are evil? Furthermore, these riches are also called His goodness; that is, they are the goodness of a God that loveth righteousness and judgment;

"He loveth righteousness and judgment: the earth is full of the goodness of the Lord." (Ps 33:5). God knows that we need these things for our survival here on earth, and David recognizing that he needed these blessings to serve God better said,

"Surely goodness *(that is, God's riches and provisions)* and mercy shall follow me all the days of my life: and I will dwell in the house of the Lord forever." (Ps 23:6). Do not try to spiritualize it. You cannot be holier than God. Accept the fact that you need them; otherwise you will die in penury. Remember, what you appreciate and respect, you attract.

A question you must answer.

Let me ask you a question. Where do you think Abraham, Isaac, Jacob, David, Solomon, and Job are, in Heaven or in Hell? If they are in heaven, that means that riches are not hindrances to righteousness.

I feel that I have to say these to destroy the myths on prosperity that have kept many Christians bound for long. The truth is that "your heavenly Father knoweth that ye need all these things *(money, clothes, food, shelter, etc)*." (Mt 6:32). What God hates and still hates is "the love of money" which He said "is the root of all evil." And not money itself!

"For the love of money *(not the possession of money)* is the root of all evil:" (1 Tim 6:10). The love of money is the root of all evil because it causes many who trust in riches to err from the faith, thereby bringing sorrow and sometimes death. Money is not to be loved but used. It is a messenger, a servant. Do not make it a lord over your life.

Why wealth and riches?

Having laid the above foundation, I will like to state that wealth is a necessary evidence of kingdom excellence. It is an undeniable proof that one is excelling. However, not knowing how to get it in the kingdom has been the bane of many Christians, so they resort to the devil. In the next few chapters, I will make you see the easy channels for kingdom prosperity. What I will be revealing to you in the next few chapters will make the enemy very angry. We will be debunking one of his greatest lies. He is free to be as angry as he wants. Your freedom is all that matters to God. Open your eyes wide and learn.

Prayer, fasting, and church attendance are not the right keys for prosperity. They can help destroy yokes and burdens, but not poverty. They can even help expose you to the keys of prosperity, but they will never break the backbone of poverty.

Let me shock you. Prophetic utterances cannot deliver you from poverty. They only show you what is possible in your life. Warring warfare with those prophesies using the right keys of the kingdom is what breaks the yoke of poverty. As you make up your mind to practice the covenant of prosperity, which is the kingdom key to abundance, I welcome you into your season of glad tidings. You shall from henceforth be a wonder to your generation in all aspects of life, amen.

Why prosperity?

Before I go into the keys of kingdom prosperity, I will like to enlighten you on the various reasons why God has decided to make you wealthy. When you do not know the reason, you may fail to satisfy the giver by your actions, and then He may decide to take away what He has blessed you with. Myles Monroe once said, "When purpose is unknown, abuse is inevitable." God will not make you wealthy so that you will brag about it, molest others with your wealth, or even throw it around, no, but that;

a. **You shall be a blessing to others**. God makes people wealthy so that they will make others wealthy too, help those in need, and be a succor to the poor. God does not desire that you should be the end point, but rather a channel of blessings, a distributor of His wealth and goodness. Divine prosperity is principally for distribution. It is only those who are willing to distribute that end up retaining God's riches. When He called Abraham, God said,

"I will bless thee, and make thy name great; and thou shalt be a blessing: and in thee shall all families of the earth be blessed" (Gen 12:2-3). To emphasize this fact, God again in Genesis chapter 22 verses 17 and 18 said, "in blessing I will bless thee, and in multiplying I will multiply thy seed...And in thy seed shall all the nations of the earth be blessed."

God always calls people so as to create channels of blessings. God blesses so that we can in turn bless our world, the kingdom, the poor, etc. You are thus enriched to enrich your world. Therefore, only distributors will continually enjoy the outpouring of God's blessings.

Channels through which you can distribute God's blessings include your usual freewill offerings and tithes, assistance to believers in the household of faith (Gal 6:10), knowing that as you help the poor, you are lending to God (Prov 19:17). Also, you should do good to all men, because only those that do good shall see good. (Ps 112:1-10).

b. **You shall help spread the gospel**. The Bible said that the gospel, "through prosperity shall be spread abroad;" (Zech 1:17).
c. You shall prove to the whole world that God is not a liar and therefore help establish His covenant on earth. See Deuteronomy 8:18

d. **Your eyes may be fixed on Him**. God knows that when you are fully provided for, the devil will not be able to deceive you again with promises of wealth and protection. In order to forestall this, He blesses you with his goodness (riches) and mercies so that you may abide in Him. (Ps 23:6).

Having therefore shown you the reason why God desires to make you rich, let us now go into the keys to this kingdom wealth.

CHAPTER TWENTY-FOUR

OFFERINGS

"Every seed is a potential forest.
If left alone or eaten it dies."

Prosperity is not a promise. It is a covenant, and it is the practice of this covenant that destroys poverty, lack and all forms of want. You cannot claim prosperity from prayers, fasting nor by faith but must practice it to see it.

In every blessing of God that comes your way, there is the **seed**, and there is the **bread**. God expects you to eat the bread, and sow the seed. Many Christians eat both the seed and the bread. This is a tragedy and the root cause of all their sufferings and financial bondages. If you fail to sow, there will always be nothing to harvest. Tithes and Offerings are some of the several ways of seed sowing.

Like every seed, the planting is the very first step. After planting, there is the need to watch over it, water it, uproot unwanted weeds, fence the garden against thieves and wide beasts, and nurture to maturity. The planted seed will then germinate, grow, mature and bear fruits.

The time it takes for the seed to mature into fruits varies from seed to seed. So are spiritual seeds. You do not harvest the day you planted. The fruits you are eating today are the seeds you sowed yesterday, and the seeds you plant today, you will eat tomorrow.

Five types of Christians.

There are five types of Christians. There are those who do not plant at all; others that plant, but on the wrong soil; those that plant, maybe on good soils but do not watch over their plantings; those that plant but abort their harvest, and those that plant, tend, and harvest at the right time.

Let us look at these groups one by one.

1. **Those that do not plant at all**. These are the people that eat both their seed and bread. This group is very common in Christendom. They believe that God does not need their offerings; and they will remind you, as if you forgot that the earth is the Lord's and the fullness thereof. Some of them believe that offerings and tithes are paid to the pastors and that giving such offerings makes the pastor to feed fat. To them, it is better to use the money than to sow into the kingdom or into the life of a pastor.

   They are totally ignorant of the need for seed sowing. Yet they pray without ceasing for financial prosperity. They pray, fast, claim prophetic utterances and even confess wealth. However, they are like a farmer who never planted any seed in his farm, but regularly goes to the farm to water, weed, and look after the farm. He even fenced the farm. At the end of the planting season, such a person will have nothing to harvest. And such watering may even cause erosion. Our confession, fasting and prayers are like watering and tending the farm. If nothing was planted, nothing grows, and at the end nothing is harvested. This means that all the efforts put into watering and tending the farm will end up being wasted efforts. Have you not heard,

"I have planted, Apollos watered; but God gave the increase"? (1 Cor 3:6). For there to be any harvest, planting must precede watering, otherwise, you may cause erosion on the field.

Therefore, **"Be not deceived; God is not mocked: for whatsoever a man soweth, that shall he also reap." (Gal 6:7).** If you sow something, you reap something, but where you sow nothing, you also reap nothing. So, plant that you may reap, and when you plant, plant good seeds not leftovers. Plant substance, for it is only when you honor God with substance and the first fruits of your increase that your barns become filled with plenty, and thy presses burst out with new wine. (Prov 3:9-10).

2. **Those that plant on wrong soil.** There are some Christians who heard that to reap, they must plant, so they planted. But the sad thing is that they planted on wrong soils. Seeds do not grow everywhere; they only grow on a good soil (Deut 12:5, 13). Any

planting on wrong soil will not yield a good harvest. Jesus even said it in the parable of the sower. Hear what he said,

"Behold, a sower went out to sow; And when he sowed, some seeds fell by the road side... Some fell upon stony places, where they had not much earth...And some fell among thorns... But others fell into good ground," (Mt 13:3-8). According to the parable, only those that fell on good ground "brought forth fruit, some an hundredfold, some sixtyfold, some thirtyfold." So planting is not all that matters. Planting in a good soil is more important. Planting on the road side, stony places and among thorns is planting on wrong soils! Maybe you have been sowing without any results. Let me ask you this simple question, **where do you sow?** For instance, where do you pay your tithe or give your offering? Is it in a place where people believe that prosperity is anti-covenant and ungodly? There for instance is not a good soil.

You can easily know a good soil. A good soil is anywhere good things are happening, where you see yourself increasing continuously is a good soil.

3. **Those that do not watch over their plantings.** These is another group of Christians who have come to the understanding that planting is good, but do not know that every planting needs to be watched over, tended to, to yield maximum harvest. In the passage above, the same seed yielded hundred,

sixty, and thirty in different hands. The difference is just a function of how good the sower watched over them.

Watching over your seed in the covenant involves keeping to the rules of the covenant. For instance, you must confess right. Be a good talker. The talking process is the watering process. Some people kill their harvest by their wrong confessions. Until your words are acceptable, your seeds will not yield their best. Do not join them in wrong talks, which destroy destiny.

Also watching over your harvest involves fighting anything that may want to abort your harvest. Such things include doubts, murmurings and complaining. Even laziness is a weed that must be removed. Be diligent in your work (Prov 22:29). God does not bless lazy men. The work of your hand is a channel for God's blessings. Be therefore a hard worker. There is a great harvest ahead, but you must protect your seed from all the adversaries of life. Hear what Paul said, **"a great door and effectual is opened unto me, and there are many adversaries." (1 Cor 16:9).** He recognized this, and therefore fought a good fight of faith. If you do not fight the adversaries, you lose the harvest. But you shall not lose your harvest in Jesus name.

4. **Those that abort their harvest**. Impatience is the commonest cause of this among Christians. They have planted, watched over their plantings, but just

before the harvest is ripe, they lose patience and lose their harvest. This group of Christians are also very common. I will like to remind such Christians that **"The Lord is not slack concerning His promise, as some men count slackness." (2 Pet 3:9).** He always makes "everything beautiful in His time:" (Eccl 3:11). God brings in the harvest when He knows that they are fully mature. This may not always coincide with when you want it, but trust God, He will never mismanage your life. Be like Abraham of the New Testament that will be said to have **"staggered not at the promise of God through unbelief...And being fully persuaded that, what he has promised, he was able also to perform."** Give God time; allow Him to do it at His own time. What would you prefer, an imperfect blessing or a perfect one? The choice is yours. Perfect blessings come only at His appointed time.

A wrong heart also aborts harvest. Remember, "The Lord searches the hearts." (Jer 17:10). God looks at the heart, and your heart determines your harvest. So have a good heart. Until your heart is right, you cannot be marked right. For instance, sow your seeds cheerfully for God loves a cheerful giver. (2 Cor 9:7, Deut 28:47-48).

Also, a wrong motive can abort harvest. The best motive for sowing in the kingdom is love. Do it out of your affection for the house of God, not to show off to the world or for recognition. Be a David of this generation. (1 Chron 29:3). If possible, sow in secret

(Mt 6:3-4). Remember any seed sown without love is a wasted seed.

5. **Those that plant, water, tend and allow for full maturation.** These are the mature Christians, who know the covenant and practice it to the full. This is where God wants you to belong. As you make up your mind to join this exalted group of mature Christians, I see as you **"goeth forth and weeping, bearing precious seed...doubtless come again with rejoicing, bearing** *your* **sheaves with** *you.*" **(Ps 126:6)** (Note: the changes are mine for emphasis).

Offering guiding rules.

Having stimulated you enough, let me show you how to plant and obtain a good harvest. Again, before you give, understand that in offering, there are dos and don'ts.

a. **God hates people appearing before him empty.** This does not mean that He expects you to come with what you do not have. No. He knows your ability per time, and every time, there is always something you can give to God, no matter how small. Just be reassured that He knows your ability. So, when you want to give, give according to your own ability. This was why He said, **"they shall not appear before the Lord empty: Every man shall give as he is able, according to the blessings of the Lord thy God which he hath given thee." (Deut 16:16-17).** Let me re-iterate the point that He knows your ability, so do not try to please Him by giving beyond your means. He is not a taskmaster, not out to ruin you but to make you. Also see Luke 12:48.

b. **Giving bad offering is worse than not giving anything at all**. In fact it is a curse! What you cannot give to your leader, please do not give it to God (Deut 17:1, Mal: 6-8).

c. **You should always give something that is useful to you**. Do not give anything that cost you nothing. (1 Chron 21:22-24).

d. **You must present your offering in a very simple fashion**. No complexities, just the way it is. Hear the wise advice of Paul, **"he that giveth, let him do it with simplicity;" (Rom 12:8).** Do not try to make it look like what it is not. That is not God's way. He already knows what you intend to give, why you are giving it, and the nature of your heart; so, allow Him to bless you by being just who you are.

e. **Jesus is watching and weighing**. Jesus is always watching and weighing your offering according to your several abilities. (Mk 12:41-44, Lk 21:1-4). You are not a giver until you give your size. Give therefore your size per time.

f. **Prayer should accompany your offering**. Do not just drop it into the basket. Pray over it. Send it on a mission. Attach a need or request to your offering. Turn it into a messenger for your harvest. Say like Jacob, **"Take I pray thee, my blessing that is brought to thee; because God hath dealt graciously with me," (Gen 33:11).**

g. **Expect a harvest**. Expect a return. Your seed is not a gift; it is a seed. It is an investment. So, expect a bountiful harvest. It is what you expect that you attract. It is your expectation not your gifts that God promised that will never be cut off (Prov. 24:14), so expect something in return.

Five reasons why you must give.

Furthermore, let me show you five reasons why you must have to give before itemizing the various channels of giving in the kingdom. This is to prepare your hearts before you give to make your giving acceptable, profitable and highly rewarding.

You ought to give because

> ➤ **It is a commandment from God**. Hear this, **"Honour the Lord with thy substance, and with the first fruits of all thine increase:" (Prov. 3:9).** Does it sound like the fifth commandment? Yes. Also, like the fifth commandment, it carries a lot of benefits, **"So shall thy barns be filled with plenty, and thy presses shall burst out with new wine." (Prov. 3:10).** If plenty is what you desire, obey this simple commandment.
> ➤ **It is more blessed to give than to receive**. (Acts 20:35). Christ gave, and today He has been exalted (2 Cor. 8:9). What do you prefer; to be a lender or a borrower, on top or beneath, first or last? Giving helps you fulfill God's plans and purposes for your life. So, give.
> ➤ **Freely you received**. (Mt 10:8). What do you have that you did not receive? The life you live is a gift, the job you are doing, the health in your body, and even the money in your pockets are all gifts from God. So

freely you received. God expects you also to freely give. Having said all these, giving has rewards.

> **When you give, you receive in return**. See what the master said, **"Give, and it shall be given unto you; good measure, pressed down, and shaken together, and running over, shall men give into your bosom. For with the same measure that ye mete withal it shall be measured to you again." (Lk 6:38).** Your giving is not wasted. It is an investment that will always bring returns. You want your blessings to run over? Then, give.

> **Scattering increases you**. This is kingdom theory. It never fails. You cannot explain it, but it is true. Hear what the wise man said, **"There is he that scattereth, and yet increaseth; and there is he that withholdeth more than is meet, but it tendeth to poverty."** This is because **"The liberal soul shall be made fat: and he that watereth shall be watered also himself." (Prov. 11:24-25).**

When you fail to give, you steal from God. And when you rob God, you walk under a curse and the devourer deals mercilessly with you. Therefore return to God that he may return unto you. Malachi said,

"Return unto me, and I will return unto you, saith the Lord of hosts. But ye said, Wherein shall we return? Will a man rob God? Yet ye have robbed me. But ye say, Wherein have we robbed thee? In tithes and offerings. Ye are cursed with a curse: for ye have robbed me, even this whole nation. Bring ye all the tithes into the storehouse, that there may be meat in

mine house, and prove me now herewith, saith the Lord of hosts, if I will not open you the windows of heaven, and pour you out a blessing, that there shall not be room enough to receive it. And I will rebuke the devourer for your sakes, and he shall not destroy the fruits of your ground; neither shall your vine cast her fruit before the time in the field, saith the Lord of hosts. And all nations shall call you blessed: for ye shall be a delightsome land, saith the Lord of hosts. (Mal 3:7-12).

Let us continue in the next chapter.

CHAPTER TWENTY-FIVE

OFFERINGS (PART 2)

"Giving prevents grieving, as
Offering prevents suffering."

There was this young man, who had everything going for him. In his place of work, he was well loved. He had two cars, a house, a plot of land, and several millions in the bank. Then, all of a sudden, everything went bad. He suffered several setbacks that he lost everything. It was then that we started asking, why? What did we find? He was a robber of God.

Before his exalted status, he was a good Christian, a member of several service groups, a lover of God, always paying his tithes and giving offerings as and when due. Then God started blessing him, and as he increased, he started having reasons why he couldn't serve God as he used to do, even his tithing became a problem and offerings were inconsistent. Several times, he admitted, he gave offerings that he himself knew were far below his new status.

Then the devil struck. Today, he has repented of his sins, asked God for forgiveness, and is gradually on his way back to the top. He has learned his lessons.

This is exactly what happens to many Christians. This shall never be your portion. May it never be said of you that you were once a big and rich man, amen.

What am I saying? Not obeying the covenant can cause misery and sorrow. Practice the covenant, not for anybody's good, but for your own good.

Results of an acceptable offering.

Let me show you the benefits of this kingdom key. Cast your mind back to the passage we read from Malachi 3:7-12. What did you notice? Apart from the benefits of service highlighted in chapter twenty-three, which are also applicable to offering (being a form of service in the kingdom), giving to God for the expansion of the gospel and for the good of the works of God has some specific benefits. Some of the benefits of giving, found in Malachi, include,

1. **Blessings rather than curses:** When you fail to give, **"Ye are cursed with a curse:"** That means that when you give you are blessed with God's blessings. And if you have not been giving before, the moment you start giving, God takes away these curses from you. Not giving God what belongs to Him incurs His wraths and curses. Do you know why? The answer is very simple. When you fail to give your tithes and offerings, you rob God. This

makes you a thief. And every thief is under a curse. The Bible calls it the curse of the thief, and it **"is the curse that goeth forth over the face of the whole earth: for every one that stealeth..."** and the victim **"shall be cut off..."** the Lord went on to say, **"I will bring it forth...and it shall enter the house of the thief..." (Zech. 5:3-4).** Have you now seen why I said that such a person is under a curse? The moment you comply, your obedience makes God to cancel the curses hanging over your head. Set yourself free today. Obey and enjoy God.

2. **Supernatural Supplies:** Once you are a giver, God has a challenge for you, **"Prove me herewith, if I will not open you the windows of heaven,"** Giving guarantees supernatural supplies. All givers are shiners. Nobody gives to God and goes down. He is a rewarder of them that diligently seek and serve Him. He is not a taskmaster, but desires to polish your destiny. As you give willingly, cheerfully, and according to your several abilities, God decorates your life with His goodness and riches.

3. **Overflowing Blessings:** Giving triggers overflowing blessings. **"I will ...pour out a blessing, that there shall not be room enough to receive it."** Giving procures overflowing, overwhelming, and infallible divine blessings. Look at Abraham, God blessed him and he became the father of many nations; Abraham blessed Isaac, and even in famine he became the envy of a whole nation; Isaac blessed Jacob, and despite ten times changes in wages, he left the house of Laban as a very rich man. The blessings of the Lord maketh rich and added no sorrow with

it. What you need is just God's blessings, and every other thing shall answer to you. Giving is the easiest means of securing this all-important blessing.

4. **Security and Protection:** Giving ensures security of all we have. God promises that with your giving, **"I will rebuke the devourer for your sakes, and he shall not destroy the fruits of your ground;"** Giving makes God your security. If God is your security, no thief can break in to steal. When God blesses you, He also preserves your blessings from the attacks of the enemy. He rebukes the devourer for your sake. He makes sure that sicknesses, deaths, thieves, etc., do not deprive you of His blessings nor prevent you from enjoying all the blessings of God in your life. Giving makes God to become your banker and defense; and is the best way to "lay up for yourself treasures in heaven, where neither moth nor rust doth corrupt, and where thieves do not break through and steal."(Mt 6:19-20).

5. **Preservation of blessings:** Giving preserves your blessings **"Neither shall your vine cast her fruit before the time in the field,"** When you give, it serves as a preservative over your blessings. Many people get blessed, but before they know it, they are no more blessed. But this is not the same with givers. Givers are forever blessed. When a giver gets pregnant, for instance, she does not miscarry; when he starts a new business, it does not bankrupt; and when he begins a trade, he does not lose his capital. He does not pursue a contract and miss it when it is about to mature. Near misses are never associated with him. Why? Because God cannot

allow the vine of a giver to cast its fruit before its time.

In addition, as we said in kingdom service, givers fulfill their days on the earth; this is also a form of not casting their fruits before their time. Look at a woman named Dorcas. She was a giver, the Bible testified of her giving, and said **"this woman was full of good works and alms deeds…"** and anyone, especially the widows, could also testify to her giving. When she died, because she was still relevant to her world, she was forced to come back to life through the ministry of a prophet, Peter (Acts 9:36-40). People who give do not die young.

6. **Evidential Blessings:** The blessings of a giver are open for all to see, as **"…all nations shall call you blessed: for you shall be a delightsome land,"** Giving makes you a living proof to your world. The blessings that accrue to you due to your giving, which are undeniable, make your world to call you blessed. You become a delight to your generation. Everyone will love you, want to be associated with you, and even pray to be like you. Giving therefore makes you a reference point.

7. **Prayer Advantage:** Kingdom service accelerates answers to prayers. However, giving gives prayers the speed of light. Concerning true givers, the Bible said, **"before they call, I will answer, and while they are yet speaking, I will hear." (Is 65:24).** This was why the prayer of Cornelius, a gentile, was given immediate attention. See the testimony

of God about him, **"A devout man, and one that feared God with all his house, which gave much alms to the people," (Acts 10:2).** In fulfillment of the above scripture from Isaiah, it was therefore not surprising that **"While Peter yet spake these words,"** before they even prayed, **"the Holy Ghost fell on all them which heard the word." (Vs 44).** Giving makes God easily accessible.

Avenues for kingdom investment.

Now let me show the avenues for kingdom investment.

a. Freewill offering (Deut. 16:6). God commands that you should not appear before Him empty.

b. Project offering. When you get involved in projects of the kingdom, you project your life to the world. Remember David and the house of God, how he prepared for it, and even vowed not to sleep until the house of His God was built. See what he said, **"Surely I will not come into the tabernacle of my house, nor go up into my bed; I will not give sleep to mine eyes, or slumber to mine eyelids, Until I find a place for the Lord, an habitation for the mighty God of Jacob." (Ps 132:3-5).** Then when you show this type of love to his projects, He will say concerning you, **"I have found..."** Then you can ask for His favour and say with boldness, **"Thou shalt arise, and have mercy upon Zion** *(me)*: **for the time to favour her, yea, the set time is come. For thy servants take pleasure in her**

stones, and favour the dust thereof." (Ps 102:13-14). And He will hear you.

But if you fail to favour the stones of Zion with your offerings, and dwell in your finished houses, you may have to re-consider your ways. Why? God will cause your heavens to be closed and inspirations shall be blocked. This will make life very difficult for you. Hear what the Bible said and change your attitude,

"Then came the word of the Lord by Haggai the prophet, saying, is it time for you, O ye, to dwell in your ceiled houses, and this (my) house is waste? Now therefore thus saith the Lord of hosts; consider your ways. Ye have sown much and bring in a little; ye eat, but ye have not enough; ye drink, but ye are not filled with drink; ye clothe you, but there is none warm; and he that earneth wages earneth wages to put it into a bag with holes. Thus saith the Lord; consider your ways."

What does He expect you to do? The Lord is saying, **"Go up to the mountain, and bring wood, and build the house; and I will take pleasure in it, and I will be glorified..."** if you fail to do this, your suffering will continue, for,

"Ye looked for much, and lo, it came to little; and when ye brought it home, I did blow upon it. Why? Saith the Lord of hosts. Because of mine house that is waste, and ye run every man

unto his own house. Therefore *(I made sure that)* **the heaven over you is stayed from dew, and the earth is stayed from her fruit.***(Because this is not yet enough)***I called for a drought upon the land, and upon the mountains, and upon the corn, and upon the new wine, and upon the oil, and upon that which the ground bringeth forth, and upon men, and upon cattle, and upon all the labour of the hands. (Hag 1:3-11).** Give to the kingdom and avoid all these calamities.

c. Giving to the less privileged. Be a new generation Job. When you give to the less privileged, you partake of the secrets of God, enjoy His presence, provisions and honour (Job 29:3-16). Remember, he that giveth to the poor, lends to God.

d. Giving to your parents. Jacob became Israel because he gave to his father, Isaac (Gen 27:1-29). When he gave to his father, Jacob obtained a blessing that flowed from the heart of the father. That marked the beginning of his exploits. When you minister to your parents, apart from the benefits highlighted above, you also enjoy divine welfare, long life, financial dominion, etc. (Eph. 6:1-3; Is. 3:10, Ex 20:12, Gen 27:28).

e. Giving to the prophets. Be like the widow of Zarephath in 1 Kings 17:9-24. While she hosted the prophet, she never lacked what to eat, and when her child fell ill and died, the prophet brought him back to life. When you give to a prophet, you receive impossible miracles and blessings like this widow of Zarephath. Above all, you shall also receive a prophet's reward

(Mt 10:41-42); which include the prayer of Paul to the Philippians, **"But my God shall supply all your need according to his riches in glory by Christ Jesus." (Phil 4:19).**

Remember, the Bible enjoins us not to forget our ministers, but to take care of them. (Gal 6:6-7, Deut. 12:19).When you minister to God's servant, you are ministering unto God. They are messengers of God, for God can do nothing except He reveals His secrets first to the prophets, His servants.(Amos 3:7). Offer to prophets and enjoy prosperity on earth. (2 Chron. 20:20)

f. Giving to strangers. Learn also to give to strangers who you see in places you go to, or who may even visit your homes. In so doing, like Abraham, you may entertain angels unawares (Heb 13:1-2). Please understand me clearly. You need to be very sensitive in the spirit to know which stranger to entertain and not. Do not be careless with strangers; they have ruined many destinies.

g. Tithes. Tithe is so important to be discussed as a concluding part of a Chapter. So, I will like us to discuss it in the very next chapter.

CHAPTER TWENTY-SIX

TITHES

When you keep God's tithes,
You live a tight life."

This is one issue that has made or marred several destinies. It has made the destinies of those that believed in it and practice it; while on the other hand, destroyed the destinies of those who believe it not. Tithing is a very serious issue in kingdom excellence. A non-tither is a mistake. He is walking in disobedience, under a curse, and in total disregard of the principles of prosperity; and so, cannot excel.

Why tithe?

Tithe is a way by which you show your understanding that there is a God up there who watches over the affairs of men. Jacob recognized this, that was why he said, **"And this stone, which I have set for a pillar, shall be God's house: and of all that thou shalt give me I will surely give the tenth unto thee." (Gen 28:22).** Even if God did not command it, which He did, won't you appreciate Him for His blessings in your life? But He, understanding the hardness of men's heart, commanded it. He said,

"Thou shalt truly tithe all the increase of thy seed, that the field bringeth forth year by year." (Deut. 14:22). Tithe is, therefore, not a once in a lifetime affair, it is a continuous activity involving all increases, whether cash or materials.

What is tithe?

Many people are still very much confused on what tithe is. Tithe is not any amount you feel like giving to God out of the much He has blessed you with. It is not a gift to God. It is not a bribe. And it is not a freewill offering. Tithe is a requirement you must fulfill for your increase to continue, it is a commandment you must obey to avoid the wrath of God, it is **the first ten percent of all your increase.** Not the last ten percent please.

Also, tithe is not fifteen or more percent and, not five percent of your increases. I hear many Christians saying that they paid a fifty, thirty, or even a one hundred percent tithe of their income. Let me state here that there is nothing like these. Tithe is tithe. A hundred percent tithe simply means a complete tithe of ten percent of all your increase. Any amount beyond this figure is freewill or sacrificial offering, as the case maybe. God's request is very simple, **ten percent only!**

Paying your tithe as, and when due shows that you recognize the source of your blessings - God. If you recognize your source, and constantly acknowledge Him,

He will never stop blessing you. Where you fail to give Him His due, He will curse your blessing. Hear what he said concerning what I have just said,

"If you will not hear, and if you will not lay it to heart, to give glory unto my name, saith the Lord of hosts, I will even send a curse upon you, and I will curse your blessings:" (Mal 2:2).

Who do you pay your tithe to?

Many people again make mistakes concerning who to pay their tithe's to. You do not pay your tithe to the beggar on the street, the widow, orphan, or destitute in the society. Neither do you pay your tithe into a social course.

You are required by God to pay your entire tithe to God and God alone. You must bring it into the storehouses of the Lord so that there will be meat in God's house (Mal 3:10). When you drop your tithe in the offering basket, you are not paying to the pastor as so many people wrongly think, but to God. And God who sees in secret will reward you openly. Your tithe should be used to solve the needs of the kingdom – that there may be meat (resources) in my house!

Who shall pay tithe?

Tithe is not just for church members alone, or those that need one favour from God or the other. Everybody is commanded to pay tithe (Mal 3:8). There are no exceptions. Pastors, deacons, ordained workers, ordinary members, all are duty bound to pay tithe. It is only after this has been done judiciously that true life really begins.

Companies, organizations and establishments can also pay tithe just as Abraham did. You can pay the tithe of your company to put your company under open heavens.

Where do you pay your tithe?

You are not expected to pay your tithe any or everywhere. Not even to any ministry, but you should pay your tithe to the ministry where you are spiritually nourished. This could be your local church. Do not give your tithe to an individual or organization. Pay your tithe in the house of God.

How is tithe paid?

Tithe, like offering, should not be paid grudgingly, but with rejoicing and a cheerful heart backed up with prayer and thanksgiving (Deut 26:1-15).

Also, when you want to pay your tithes, delay is not acceptable. I have said it before that tithe is the first ten not the last ten percent of all increases. God forbids any delay, least the devil tempts you to spend it and you do. Hear His candid advice,

"Thou shalt not delay to offer the first of thy ripe fruits, and of thy liquors:" (Ex 22:29). It is either the first or nothing. Any offer that falls short of this requirement is not acceptable.

Having said this, peradventure you traveled out of your station, and the need arises for you to pay tithe, what do you do? Simple – separate your tithe from the increase, eat the bread, sow the seed, but keep your tithe in a safe place. On your return, promptly pay your tithe. You can also pay via online bank transactions and transfers. This is acceptable!

Boosters.

There is a grace for giving. You need this grace of giving to be able to pay your tithe as and when due (2 Cor 8:7-8). Pray for this grace, and as you sincerely desire to have this grace, I see God baptizing you afresh with the Holy Spirit and with power to do exploits for the kingdom of our God.

Do you know that our covenant fathers paid tithes? Abraham paid tithe to Melchizedek, priest of the most high God (Gen 14:20, Heb 7:4-10); Hezekiah restored tithing in Israel (2 Chron 31: 4-6), and even Jesus while speaking about the credentials of the Pharisee, mentioned tithing when He said, "I give tithes of all that I possess." (Lk18: 12). In other words, it is a vital point in worship, even though the Pharisee was not doing many other things that were required of him.

Benefits.

Look at all the blessings of giving and kingdom service again. Tithing procures all of them, and even adds extra. Join the true excellence club today. Be a tither and your life will never be the same again. Ask other tithers what life is like, and you will be amazed when you discover what you have been missing all these years. As you take the right step today, I see the God of restoration visiting you to restore all that the locust, caterpillar, cankerworm and palmerworm hath eaten.

CHAPTER TWENTY-SEVEN

SACRIFICE

*"Sacrifice is the narrow gate
That leads to astonishing blessings"*

Sacrifice is a price that everyone who desires kingdom excellence must pay once and again. My Bishop calls it "the price for significance." Sacrifice has been in vogue from the time of Adam and Eve. Remember God Himself had to slaughter an animal to clothe the naked two. He could have created a cloth for them from nowhere or even called on the spider to provide a silk clothing so as to cover them. But His plan was not just to cover them, but also to atone for their sins. So He carried out the first ever recorded sacrifice.

Also, Cain and Abel sacrificed. I could imagine them asking their parents who their grandfather and grandmother were. I believe that Adam, going by their probing questions, must have told them all he knew about himself and God, how God used to visit them in the cool of the evenings, how God warned them to eat everything in the garden except of the tree of good and evil, how they disobeyed and thus lost God's daily communion and fellowship, and then how God killed an animal to make a coat of skin for them.

These young and intelligent boys, full of insight, must have decided to do what God did, but this time around to offer it to God for a return fellowship with Him. This they did, and God was moved, accepted Abel's sacrifice because it involved blood, but rejected Cain's sacrifice because no blood was shed. This was so significant with God that after Cain killed Abel; Abel's sacrifice was still speaking for him even in death.

Noah sacrificed after the flood. Abraham sacrificed at God's instructions. His several sacrifices led to the covenant that you and I are enjoying today. Isaac, Jacob, Jephthah, David, Solomon, etc., all sacrificed to God at one time or the other. Solomon's sacrifice was another very thoughtful one. Out of love for God, he sacrificed a thousand burnt offerings upon an altar in one single day. This brought God down, and He gave the young king an open cheque, **"Ask what I shall give thee." (1 Kgs 3:5).** By this single sacrifice, he became the wisest king of his time, the richest, the most popular and the only king in Israel that never fought a war throughout his reign as he had peace round about him. All these were obtained at the altar of sacrifice.

What then is a sacrifice?

Sacrifice means denying yourself something very important for a course you desire. Today, it no more involves the art of killing an animal and pouring the blood on an altar. That used to be the case before Christ. But with the coming of Christ,

His death on Calvary and resurrection, such sacrifices are no more required. For Christ has paid the price once and for all. Blood sacrifices are no longer relevant.

Modern day sacrifice, therefore, refers to **satisfying God first at the expense of your immediate needs for tomorrow's gains.** This is how I see it. That is, submitting something very important to God for something more important from Him; doing without something you love so much for a cause you believe in; forgoing a precious item for the decoration that comes from God; giving God an extra-ordinary gift in expectation for undeniable blessings. Giving God uncommon gift so as to receive uncommon reward.

Usually, sacrifices are not convenient. They involve doing some uncommon things for uncommon blessings. It involves going out of your way to show God that you really trust in Him, that your trust is not in riches but knowing that He is too good to fail or mismanage your life; that is putting every bit of your trust on the Almighty.

Sacrifice is a way of telling God that you understand that all true riches come from Him and Him alone. It is letting God see how faithful you are with the little blessings He has given you. God desires that we pass this 'faithfulness' test so that He may know whether we are trustworthy, as in the case of Abraham (Gen 22:1-18). Until we pass this test, He cannot trust us. Every child of God has an equal glorious destiny, but the marks we score in this test determine how colourful our destiny finally becomes. The higher the score, the more glorious the future.

Why Sacrifices?

1. God made and is always making sacrifices for men. He desires that we reciprocate His acts to prove our faithfulness.

2. God does not lack blessings to give to His children, neither does He have any problem blessing people, but His greatest problem is retaining them afterwards. For, **"no good thing will He withhold from them that walk uprightly." (Ps 84:11).** He chooses those to bless based on their trustworthiness. And sacrifice is a major criterion for judging trustworthiness.

3. The altar of sacrifice is the altar of change, a place of total turn around. So anytime you desire a forceful change, make a sacrifice. Every man of sacrifice is a symbol of unexplainable testimonies. If prosperity is our desire, sacrifice is the way to it. This has been the experiences of many of us till date.

When sacrifice is properly offered, it procures,

➢ A change of status. See Solomon's case. His sacrifice made him the envy of his generation.

➢ Release of undeniable blessings that always commands envy. Solomon's wealth commanded envy and is still commanding envy to this day.

➢ Establishes your superiority. Elijah with the prophets of Baal. His acceptable sacrifice made all around him to wonder at him and to agree to serve his God. Even when he decided to slay the four hundred and fifty prophets of Baal, no body raised an objection (1 Kgs 18:22-40).

➢ Removal of curses. Noah is a good example. After the flood, he sacrificed to God, and the Bible recorded that God smelled a good savour and said, **"I will not again curse the ground…" (Gen 8:21).** Acceptable sacrifices save destinies from curses.

➢ Generational blessings. Abraham's sacrifice secured blessings that even we, the adopted sons of Abraham, are enjoying today. God told him after his sacrifice, **"By myself have I sworn…That in blessing I will bless thee, and in multiplying I will multiply thy seed as the stars of the heaven…and thy seed shall possess the gates of their enemies; And in thy seed shall all the nations of the earth be blessed;" (Gen 22:16-18).** Jesus Christ came from the lineage of Abraham, from the tribe of Judea. Today, there is no nation of the world that is not feeling the impact of the coming of Christ and enjoying the benefits of the breakthrough science of Israel. Truly this covenant has been fulfilled.

➢ Sacrifice accelerates prayer answers. After slaying all the prophets of Baal, Elijah prayed a prayer requesting that no rain shall fall, and God honoured his prayer. No wonder the Psalmist said, **"The Lord hear thee in the day of trouble…Remember all thy offerings, and accept thy burnt sacrifice." (Ps 20:1,3).**

➢ Turns captivities around. Jacob's captivity was turned around at the altar of sacrifice. Remember after he stole his brother's blessings, he became a fugitive and ran towards Laban's house. But the moment he raised an altar for the Lord and promised to pay tithe of everything, God gave him divine direction and his life took a new turn for good (Gen 28:22).

➤ Anytime the going gets tough, raise an altar of sacrifice. Remember the children of Israel were always sacrificing to God before every major battle. The Lord is still the same. He has not changed. He is **"the same yesterday, and today, and forever." (Heb 13:8).**

➤ Sacrifice commits God to your welfare.

➤ Sacrifice makes God your security and your avenger. For Abel even after his death, his sacrifice was still speaking for him.

Sacrifices are weighed.

Sacrifices are not usually measured by volume, but per value. It is a sacrifice only if it is a concentrated giving unto the Lord, offered for a forceful turn around. Many Christians are totally ignorant of this. God values your sacrifice based on how much discomfort it caused you. Make your sacrifices meaningful and valuable.

CHAPTER TWENTY- EIGHT

THANKSGIVING

"Anything you take for granted gets grounded;
Anything you fail to appreciate depreciates;
Anything you fail to thank God for, you will soon lack."

The last part of the above statement I learned in a very hard way. I came back from a church retreat only to discover that my taps were dry, very dry. This was actually the very first time such a thing was happening. I asked God why? But He did not answer me immediately. For several days the situation continued. All the while I had to buy water from water sellers. A few weeks later, while wondering why the tap is yet to be restored, God spoke and said,

"Now, let me tell you why there is no water. You failed to appreciate it because it was always there at your beck and call. You failed to thank me for it. So how does it feel not to have it?"

I was stupefied that God took notice of such 'small things' and then apologized. Thank God I did, otherwise who knows how much longer I would have stayed without water.

He restored it after a whole month. I choose to write on this key because it is the only key that can guarantee you a true success, sustain the success, and make sure that your blessings are neither cursed nor depreciated. A thankful man is the only person qualified for God's blessings.

Why thanksgiving?

Thanksgiving is spiritual yeast for increase. It is a catalyst for divine interventions. No blessing increases until there is a certified thanksgiving for the previous provision. Nobody makes it big in the kingdom without thanksgiving. Murmuring and complaining destroy, not only the blessings, but also the blessed; therefore **"Neither murmur ye, as some of them also murmured, and were destroyed of the destroyer." (1 Cor 10:10).** Thanksgiving is the way out.

When you thank God for His omnipresent nature, He presents His manifest presence; if you thank Him for His manifest presence, He shows you His works, and when you thank Him for His initial works, he completes what he started. Thanking God always keeps your tanks of blessings full.

Maybe you have already started applying the keys given in the twenty-seven previous chapters of this book in your life, and God has already started doing you good. If you fail in this key, **"If ye will not hear, and if ye will not lay it to heart, to give glory unto my name, saith the Lord of hosts, I will even send a curse upon you, and I will curse your blessings:" (Mal 2:2).** I choose to repeat this quotation because of its great importance. I enjoin you therefore to, **"In everything give thanks: for this is the will of God in Christ Jesus concerning you."** **(1Thess 5:18).**

Moreover, **"We are bound to thank God always..."** **(2 Thess 1:3).** Whether it is convenient or not, whether we feel like it or not, whether we believe that God has answered us or is yet to answer us, we are bound to give Him thanks. Even if you do not want to thank God because of what you stand to gain from it, which I think you really need, then do it because it is good. The Psalmist said, **"It is a good thing to give thanks unto the Lord, and to sing praises unto thy name, O most High:" (Ps 92:1).**

All men of excellence are thanks-givers. Christ was a constant thanks giver. He thanked God when He was about to feed the multitudes before breaking the bread and sharing the fishes (Mt 15:16,Mk 8:6,); and He even thanked God at Lazarus' tomb before calling on the dead man to come forth (Jn 11:41).

Paul is another great man who built his ministry around thanksgiving. It is not unusual to hear him say, "We give thanks to God always..." (1 Thess1: 2). While advising Christians worldwide, in addition to the passages from Thessalonians cited above, he said, **"Be careful for nothing; but in everything by prayer and supplication with thanksgiving let your requests be made known unto God." (Phil 4:6).** Prayers that are not underlined and sealed with thanksgiving are not likely to be answered.

The value of thanksgiving: A personal experience.

You expect thanks from people for every simple favour you offer. Imagine how you will feel if your son, daughter, or even a friend finishes eating your food, washed his/her hands and leaves your place, maybe to go and play, without saying 'thank you'. Or you have just risked your life to rescue a man from the wreckage of a car accident, cleaned him up, and then, he looks up and down the road and walks away. How will you feel? I guess very bad.

I had a taste of what I am telling you about firsthand. That was the day I truly appreciated the value of thanksgiving. I know that my wife may not like to see this story repeated in this segment of the book, but I want to tell you about it as this story will definitely bless somebody, and that person is you.

It was a few weeks to our Christian wedding. Our traditional wedding took place two months before this event. All savings were gone – as it was not even much going by my income at that time. We were looking unto God for the finances for the wedding as my wife, then my fiancée, was in school.

A month to our wedding, I got my monthly salary. What a relief. It was about twenty-two thousand naira (about 200 USD then). I removed my tithe of two thousand, two hundred naira; and sent the remaining to her with an additional two hundred naira I got from my savings to make it twenty thousand naira. I asked her to use it to start preparing for the wedding the coming month. I was to trust God solely for my meals, transport fare and money for other essentials for the entire month.

Then, like a hero who has done the impossible and made the supreme sacrifice; I jubilantly and expectantly called my wife and told her that I have sent the money to her. What was I expecting? Big thank you or maybe a hug over the phone. But what did I get? **"It won't be enough"** How bad I felt.

You know what? She asked me how much the money was and when I told her, instead of showing gratitude, she told me that it was not going to be enough. I was deeply pained. What pained me more was the fact that she knew how much I was earning at that time. This incident made me to go to God in prayers, whether I was really marrying the person he prepared for me. Let me tell you the truth, I had some sleepless nights asking God the above question.

A few days later I made a decision that saved me from the trouble. I decided to wait for her next call. I also decided that if when she called, she failed to show appreciation for the money I sent to her, that I would call off the wedding. The fact that we are married today means that she did say thanks as when next she did call, before even saying anything, she said 'Thanks'. It was then I knew that truly she was my wife.

I have told you this story to make you understand what ingratitude could cause. Maybe you have had a related experience. If I, a human being who cannot even lay any claim on the money I sent to her could feel the way I did, imagine how God feels when we fail to show Him that we are grateful for all He has done, is doing and will yet do for us.

We have enough reasons to thank him.

"O give thanks unto the Lord, for He is good:" (Ps 107:1). Give Him thanks at least for all His benefits towards you, especially concerning your sins that He forgave, thy diseases that he healed, thy life that He has redeemed from destruction, His tender mercies and loving kindness with which He has crowned your life, thy mouth that He has satisfied with good things of life, thy youth that He always renews, and His judgment and vengeance against all your enemies (Ps 103:2-6). Thank Him!

If you have no other reason to thank Him, thank Him because you can still breathe and is alive. Are there not people younger than you who are dead? Are there not people who were holier than you who are no more in the faith? Are there not people who were more hardworking that are poorer than you? Are there not people more careful than you who are victims of one accident or the other? Are there not people more beautiful than you who are not married? Are there not people more qualified than you who are jobless? Are there not people with better brains who had no chance to go to school? Are there not people far better than you who are sick, homeless, hungry, stagnated, afflicted, etc.? Are there not people more masculine (or feminine) than you who are childless? **What do you have that you have not received?**

Thank Him so that He may preserve your blessings, give you more and exalt your horn like the horn of a unicorn, anoint you with fresh oil, make your eyes see your desire for your enemies come true, make you flourish like a palm tree and like a cedar in Lebanon, and make you remain fruitful even in very old age. This He will do to show that he is upright and that there is no unrighteousness in Him (Ps 92:1; 10-15).

Always remember, that no matter your age, you have your age mates in the grave. And no matter your present condition, there are people who envy you and are praying to be just like you or where you are. Be grateful. Give thanks for everything and in everything. As my Bishop will always say, if you can think enough, you will find enough reason to thank God. So, think and thank God always.

This is the final vital force for kingdom excellence. It serves as the icing on the cake. Until it is applied, the job is yet incomplete.

CHAPTER TWENTY-NINE

TAKE A CHANCE

"Nothing happens until you make it happen"
Now that you have reached here, I am very glad. I know that you must have learned one or two things you never knew, have re-enforced your knowledge of issues and been reminded of things you may have forgotten. But all these will only be head knowledge if you stop at just knowing them.

I therefore present to you the very last key in this book. I call it; **Take a chance.**

Take a chance and move forward,
Take a chance and make a change
Take a chance and save your destiny
Take a chance and enjoy God.

You will remain where you were before you read this book, if you fail to take a chance. For the sake of your dreams and dependents, kindly take a chance.

I spoke to a friend and asked him to help publish this book under his label. But he said no. His reason was that he

271

only publishes very popular books, which has been tried in the market and found marketable. He was not willing to go into the publication of a completely new book, because he may lose his investment.

He is typical of many people. Are you like him? Having read this book till now, you seem to me to be a man who love God, and wish to take every step possible to get to the highest level in life, God's way. Your desire is very good. But until you take a step out of your old ways and plunge completely into a new way, the excellent road, you may not go very far.

So, take a chance.

You may also be a typical human being who is afraid to invest where the soil is not too fertile, protected and secure. You love to play it safe so to say, living within a safe jacket, doing the conventional things. This to me is not the best. It is never the road to the topmost top.

Great men are said to do often what small men hardly do. They do what mean men consider impossible, stupid or even foolish. They do things that other people fail to do. They take chances, they take risks. Only those willing to take a chance can get to the top.

A great man of God said, **"It is risky not to take risk."** A good businessman is somebody who is willing to do all it takes – God's way – to get to the top. And I know that nobody gets to the top being a second fiddle.

So, take a chance.

Time and chance happeneth to them all." (Eccl 9:11) What we do with our time and chance, determines to a great extent what happens to our destiny.

Imagine what could have happened to the following people if they had not taken chances.

Noah. God called him, maybe in a vision, dream, or trance. Based on this call, he took a step. A risky step you must admit. For 120 years he built an ark. Many mocked, ridiculed, and insulted him, but he was not deterred. Imagine what could have happened to him and his family if he had out of fear and uncertainty failed to take a chance. They would have all died in the flood. Would he have blamed God? I know that God has been speaking to you from the onset of this book. What is He asking you to do? Do it.

Take a chance now!

Abraham. God also called him when he was 75 years old to leave his father's house, friends, relations and inheritance to an unknown place. He took a chance. He was told to circumcise all male children in his house, he obeyed. He nearly even killed his son, Isaac, just because he believed that he heard God. Where would Abraham have been without these risky steps today? Maybe he would have died a barren man, maybe very poor, maybe a nameless person just like most of us. But he took risky steps, and these transformed his life and generations.

Is there any area of barrenness in your life; are there unproductive ventures? Then open yourself up for divine ministration. When He speaks, please do it. Do not try to explain it away.

Take a chance.

Moses. While taking care of his father-in-law's sheep, saw something that attracted him, a special fire in the bush. He decided to turn aside and look. Then he heard a voice. He took a risk, left his safe haven in Jethro's house, and went back to a place where they were looking for him to kill him. At the end of the day, he came out victorious. God even made him a god unto Pharaoh (Ex 7:1). But for his risky step, he would have died a fugitive in an unknown land, unknown, unsung, and uncelebrated. Are you in need of divine direction? God is speaking. Be sensitive. When you hear, take a chance.

David. He was sent to see to the welfare of his brothers at the war front. There he saw a giant insulting the armies of his Lord. He decided to take a risk. He saw a promise while others saw a problem; he saw an opportunity while others saw an opponent; and he saw a stepping-stone, while others saw a stumbling block. He went for it. He came out victorious, and today the whole world is still celebrating his exploits. What could have happened to him if he had not taken this risk? Where could he have ended? As a shepherd boy all his life. But he did an uncommon thing and obtained an uncommon result.

Are you facing any obstacle right now? Is there any challenge before you that looks so insurmountable? Move ahead; take a step, tackle it.

Take a chance.

Gideon, Deborah, Samson, Jephthah, Rehab, etc. all saw opportunities, took risks, and today are named in the world hall of faith with other great men and women of God. Take a chance.

In the New Testament, the list continues.

The Apostles. They were called by a man that had no name, no home, no occupation, no family inheritance, and no visible resources; but they followed. For three whole years they were with Him. They took a risk. They left their families, occupations, possessions, etc. to follow Him. Today we are still celebrating them. Otherwise, who could have heard of Peter, John, Mathew, Luke, Paul, etc. if they had failed to take the chance they took? Your guess is as good as mine. Is any opportunity staring you in the face right now which seems risky; go to God in prayers. If He says, "Go ahead." Please do go ahead. He will never misdirect you.

Take a chance.

In the world today, there are many people who took dare risks, and because of these risks, they have become celebrities worldwide. Do you remember the **Wright brothers**? They chose to go against the opinion of the world council of scientists. Today, they are the toast of all airplane builders.

What of **Bill Gates**? He took a risk with Microsoft. Many people saw the opportunity, but never used it, even people he shared his dream with, dissociated from his dream. Today, most of them are regretting, but Bill Gates is smiling home daily with his millions and is still one of the richest men in the whole world.

Why am I saying all these things? Life without a risk is a risky one. Risks taking make stars. Nobody makes it to the top without adequately utilizing his chances, if and when they come.

I think that you too should come out of your safe walls, and fish in the deep waters of life. You have fished in the shallow waters for too long.

You may even have made it big, but there is a place called forward; you may be rich and great, but there is a place called very rich and very great where people will be forced to envy you, just like Isaac.

Remember, **"Time and chance happeneth to them all."**

I have a suggestion to make. Take a chance.

Put into practice all that you have learnt from this book, and all that the Spirit has been ministering to you since you started reading this book. And your arrival at the top will become a reality. Remember, it is not he that heard, or read that is blessed, but he that is able to do all he has heard and read. Therefore, **"Be ye doers of the word, and not hearers only, deceiving your own selves." (James 1:22).** It is only when you implement all you have heard and read from this book that you will be qualified for kingdom excellence, make your way prosperous and have good success (Joshua 1:8).

You will only benefit from this book if you put into practice what you have learnt.

Take a chance now, take it today.

CHAPTER THIRTY

UNTIL YOU ARE SAVED, YOU ARE NOT SAFE

Having spent your precious time reading this book, I congratulate you. It shows that you are truly desirous of excellence in life and ministry. And your expectation shall not be cut off.

There is something else I must show you. Let us go to the book of Psalms. Hear this, **"The earth is the Lord's, and the fullness thereof; the world, and they that dwell therein. For he hath founded it upon the seas, and established it upon the floods. Who shall ascend into the hills of the Lord? Or who shall stand in his holy place? He that hath clean hands, and a pure heart; who hath not lifted up his soul unto vanity, nor swore deceitfully. He shall receive blessing from the Lord..."** (Ps 24:1-5).

The above scripture informs us that;

- The earth is the Lord's and the fullness thereof. Thus wealth, riches, happiness, joy, peace, etc. all belong to God. To excel in life, one has to obtain the things of life from God Himself.

- Even you that dwell in the earth belong to God. You do not own yourself, God does. You are accountable to your master all the time. When you fail to do this, you risk the master's punishment.

- Who shall ascend unto the hills of the Lord, or stand in His holy place? That is, who is qualified for kingdom excellence or to enjoy His numerous blessings? Who is qualified for divine helps, direction and supernatural supplies? Who will the Lord shield all around with His favour? The Bible answers and said,

- He that hath clean hands: hands clean of sin, clean of iniquity and immorality.

- He that hath a pure heart: heart that is pure of evil and devilish thoughts, heart that is panting after God and His kingdom.

- He, who hath not lifted up his soul unto vanity: he that is content with the blessings of God per time, who is neither envious, jealous nor is bitter towards others because of the blessings of the Lord in their lives. He who does not love money or the things of this world. He whose mind is stayed on God.

- He who hath not sworn deceitfully: he who has not given false evidence against his neighbour, nor sworn deceitfully, falsely, wrongly and for material or worldly gains.

When and only when you have been found faithful in all these shall the blessings of God be released unto you. To be found faithful, therefore, I present to you the road to kingdom faithfulness; Salvation.

The blessings of the Lord, which procure kingdom excellence, come only to those with excellent minds. Remember the testimony of Daniel, they said concerning him, **"For as much as an excellent spirit, and knowledge, and understanding...were found in the same Daniel," (Dan 5:12).**

This spirit of excellence resides only in those **"in whom the spirit of the holy gods;"** is found; that is, those that have the mind of Christ (1 Cor 2:16). This mind is the heritage of those that have given their lives to Jesus Christ; who have publicly declared that Christ is their Lord and personal saviour.

Once you have this excellent spirit, like Daniel, you excel in all things. Thus, kingdom excellence is not a product of struggling, but a product of wisdom arising from an excellent spirit, which quickens the mind of the person. Make therefore no mistake about it; as long as you are outside Christ, your mind is too poor to achieve the kind of excellence we are talking about here.

Moreover, a life without Christ is a life full of crisis; so

    Stop the pains now
    Stop the tears now
    Stop the suffering now
    Stop the struggling now

You have suffered enough. Accept Jesus Christ and enjoy peace, rest and happiness round about you now and always. Yielding your life to God is therefore not a loss, but an all-time gain and for high level profiting.

What else?

What other reason do I have why you must give your life to God? Romans 3:23 said, **"For all have sinned, and come short of the glory of God."**

Romans 6:23 said, **"For the wages of sin is death; but the gift of God is eternal life through Jesus Christ our Lord."**

Accept and receive this gift, for John 1:12 said, **"But as many as received him, to them gave he power to become the sons of God, even to them that believe on his name."**

Now that you have believed, confess Him. For Romans 10:9-10 said, **"That if thou shalt confess with thy mouth the Lord Jesus, and shalt believe in thine heart that God hath raised Him from the dead, thou shalt be saved. For with the heart man believeth unto righteousness; and with the mouth confession is made unto salvation.** If you have made up your mind to accept Jesus Christ as your Lord and personal saviour, say this simple prayer with me, believing every single word of it:

Almighty Father, I come to You just as I am. I know that I cannot help myself. I have sinned against You in thoughts, words and deeds. Now, I have made up my mind to forsake my old ways. Forgive me my sins and deliver me from the power of sin and death. Today, Lord, I accept You as my Lord and Saviour. Cancel my name from the book of death and accept me into the kingdom of Your dear son, Jesus Christ. Baptize me with the grace to run this new race of life with You. Establish me in Your ways, and turn my weaknesses into strength. Thank You for changing and accepting me, and making me a child of God, in Jesus mighty name, Amen.

Now you are born again. Welcome into the club of kingdom stars. You will not fail God, your friends or yourself.

To build a solid foundation in God, look for a complete Bible, read it, as often as you can and as you read, God will be revealing Himself more and more to you. Also look for a good Bible believing church and join. You can also ask the Holy Spirit to direct you to a good church where you can fellowship regularly.

See you one of these days in a Christian assembly, or better still, in heaven.

Remain blessed.

WHEN....

- ❖ When you put Gods Word to work, God Works wonders in your life
- ❖ When you return to God, God returns all you have lost to you
- ❖ When you release your seed to God, God releases his blessings to you
- ❖ When you believe in him, He makes you to become like him
- ❖ When you appear before him, He cause every evil to disappear from you
- ❖ When you sing unto him, He gives you a song of thanksgiving and makes you a testimony for all to see
- ❖ When you hear his Word, He makes people to listen to your word
- ❖ When you have a song of praise, He slays all your enemies
- ❖ When you give him the glory due to him, He fills your life with his glory
- ❖ When you behold his altar, He alters your life ministry and destiny
- ❖ When you praise him, He raises you to your next levels

- When you discover your destiny in God, He uncovers your glory on earth
- When you hand over your life to him, He hands back an enviable life to you
- When you sojourn with God, good things sojourn with you
- When you dwell with God in his house; peace, mercy and grace swell up in you
- When you encounter destiny, God gives you blessings to count
- When you turn to God, He gives you a turnaround
- When you engage His mysteries, He makes you a master in the affairs of life
- When you rest in God, He dismantles every resistance against your destiny
- When you stop at His Word, you become unstoppable in life
- When you create a conducive atmosphere for God to manifest, God makes you a manifestation on earth
- When your praise becomes unstoppable, your turnarounds become unstoppable and ceaseless
- When you praise Him, He reveals Himself to you
- When your light comes, your level changes
- When you see well, you go further and faster
- When you open up to God, He opens up your destiny
- When you know God, you do exploits
- When you highly exalt Him, He exalts you on earth
- When you do not deprive God your praise, He will not deprive you of his agenda for your life
- When you lift your hands to praise him, He lifts you to your next level of blessings

- ❖ When you rest in God, He gives you rest all around
- ❖ When you thank him for his blessing, He makes your tank full of his blessings
- ❖ When you remember the past, He reorganizes the future
- ❖ When you follow Him and His word, good things follow you and overtake you
- ❖ When you welcome God into your life, you also welcome His gift, packages, and visitations
- ❖ When you honor Him, He makes you an honor on the earth
- ❖ When you give God your all, all of God will answer to you
- ❖ When you give Him your best, He makes the rest your best
- ❖ When you encounter His light, IT enlightens your destiny and lightens your burdens
- ❖ When you laugh at life burdens, men will laugh with you at your testimony
- ❖ When you present your offerings to God, your present financial suffering will be destroyed
- ❖ When you review the approach, joy returns with better and improved results
- ❖ When you see it, you are qualified to taste it
- ❖ When you obey his command, He makes you a commander in the affairs of life
- ❖ When you love him, He lavishes you with his blessings and presents
- ❖ When you wait on Him, He Wets you with his favor, mercy and grace
- ❖ When you labour to the end, you end up celebrated, glorified and rewarded

- When you recognize his previous acts, He qualifies you for the next
- When you are joyful, you are sign-full and wonderful
- When you hear His voice, He makes you a voice on earth
- When you recognize His messenger of good news, He ransoms you out of every mess
- When you are illuminated by His word, you reign in the affairs of life
- When you give Him high praises, He delivers high level testimonies
- When you discover your destiny in Christ, you cannot live ever again as a destitute
- When you discover your call, you enter your glory and virtue
- When you run into him, your future cannot be ruptured
- When you give him your everything, you remain resourceful
- When you connect with His Words, you collect your destiny and testimonies
- When you pursue God, you return with victory and blessing
- When God remembers you, He embarrasses you with amazing visitations
- When you do NOTHING, you see nothing, and nothing happens

LET'S KEEP IN TOUCH

Thank you for taking out time to read this book. Is the time well spent? You will gain more by applying the various keys to issues of life. Daily use of these keys will make living more interesting, impactful and refreshing. Do not stop until you arrive at your vision. Try to read the book over and over again as insight improves with repeated exposures.

I am sure you must have gained one or two things from the book. Let's keep in touch.

I want to know how the book affects and impacts your life – career, marriage, academics, business, spirituality, and finances. Let's keep in touch.

I want to know the things you changed, habits you altered and risks you took; and what the results were after a few days, weeks, months and years. So, let's keep in touch.

I want to know the way the book affects your ministry, mentorship programs and trainings. What the outcome and benefits of using the key in others are. Let's keep in touch.

You can reach me on +2348096083335, pastorexcellence@gmail.com or via my blog www.obinnaoleribe.com

Let's go out there and excel as we remain in touch.

God bless you.

ABOUT THE AUTHOR

Dr Obinna O Oleribe was born into the Anglican Communion, but his search for the truth brought him into Living Faith Church Worldwide where he was ordained a Pastor in July 2008. He is a public health consultant with five fellowships including FRCP and FWACP, a doctorate degree in public health, three master's degrees in public health and business administration, and two bachelor's degrees in pharmacology, and medicine and surgery. He is a multiple award (academic and non-academic) winner. He currently works as a Chief Executive Officer of Excellence and Friends Management Care Center (EFMC) Abuja as well as oversees several other business interests including Modern Health Hospital, Centre for Family Health Initiative, and Excellence and Friends Management Consult. He serves as the West African Consultant to BroadReach Consulting LLC. He is married with wonderful children.

Printed in the United States
By Bookmasters